15-Minute
Vegan Meals

15-Minute
Vegan Meals

60 Delicious Recipes for
Fast & Easy Plant-Based Eats

Janet Gronnow
founder of Munch Meals by Janet

PAGE STREET
PUBLISHING CO.

PAGE STREET
PUBLISHING CO.

First published in 2022 by
Page Street Publishing Co.
27 Congress Street, Suite 1511
Salem, MA 01970
www.pagestreetpublishing.com

Distributed by Macmillan, sales in Canada by The Canadian Manda Group.

26 25 24 23 22   1 2 3 4 5

ISBN-13: 978-1-64567-532-7
ISBN-10: 1-64567-532-7

Library of Congress Control Number: 2021938431

Cover and book design by Molly Kate Young for Page Street Publishing Co.
Photography by Janet Gronnow

Printed and bound in the United States of America

To my dear mom and dad, and my loves Dan, Julia, & Tom

Table of Contents

Introduction

Hi there, and welcome to my cookbook! I can't express how happy I am that you're here, and I am excited to have you joining me in exploring the possibilities of quick, delicious, plant-based cooking.

My venture into plant-based cooking began four years ago, quite suddenly, really. I became aware of the positive impact of the plant-based approach to food, from the ethical, environmental, and health perspectives. And because I've been obsessed with cooking since I was a child, I had hoped to dive into vegan recipe creation with the greatest of ease. Simple, right? Well, let's just say my very first plant-based meals were pretty dismal. I didn't really know what I was doing, and I thought I was supposed to eat tofu at every meal. But with some practice and a whole lot of veggies and flavorful ingredients, I quickly realized that vegan food can be awesome. I want to help you skip that period of awkwardness that I had in the beginning. Or, if you have been eating plant-based meals for a while, this fast-cooking approach can have your back when you don't feel like, or aren't able to, spend much time in the kitchen.

I aim to create meals that both vegans and non-vegans will find satisfying and enjoyable. My hope is that you feel confident in serving these meals to all of your friends and family, whether they're vegan or not. As the only plant-based eater in my extended family, I have had some practice in creating meals where even my husband won't question where the meat is (and trust me, that's saying something). Because the focus is to make these meals super satisfying, filled with nourishing ingredients, and made simply, this collection of recipes can be a resource that you can come back to again and again.

While everyone's reasons for eating plant-based meals are different, whether you're dabbling or it's your predominant approach, there are so many ways to make it exciting and flavorful. From hearty salads, soups, and sandwiches, to pasta, curry, tacos, and warm plates, this cookbook includes it all. Whether you're mainly looking for speedy meal ideas, or for some inspiration with plant-based or vegan cooking, I hope that you will find many favorite recipes here that you can enjoy yourself and with your loved ones.

Janet Grannon

The 15-Minute Approach

How to Cook Strategically for Delicious Plant-Based Food in a Short Amount of Time

My goal with this cookbook is to give you tons of savory, flavorful, and comforting dinner options where you can think to yourself, *I have nothing made to grab from the fridge. And I'm hungry. But 15 minutes from now, I'll have a delicious meal, ready to enjoy.*

In this book, there's inspiration from a variety of cuisines. While these recipes use preparations that are not traditional—they use many shortcuts and fusions—they are a simple and fast way to pull in ingredients from different global cultures to thoroughly enjoy them. I hope that you find some new favorite ingredients along the way, and even some new ways to prepare familiar ingredients.

To that end, I aimed to make the recipes in this book cover a variety of classics, but with a twist, and also use ingredient combinations that you may not have seen before. Some recipes might seem like they have more ingredients than you'd expect in a 15-minute cookbook, but you'll usually be adding them all into one pot, many at the same time, so that they can bring a great flavor pop as they cook together in short order.

I've tried to use widely accessible ingredients that you can use again and again, and almost all of the ingredients are used in more than one recipe. There are a lot of examples where you can use the remainder of certain ingredients from one recipe to make a subsequent meal. For example, you won't need a full can of coconut milk for the Creamy Carrot, Zucchini, & Olive Pasta (page 33), but you can use the remainder of it in the Creamy Mushroom, Chickpea, & Sun-Dried Tomato Soup (page 90), or in the Sun-Dried Tomato Alfredo Penne with Broccoli (page 30). And for the canned crushed tomatoes needed for the Smoky Pinto Bean, Mushroom, & Tomato Soup (page 97), you can use the rest of the can for the Hearty Black-Eyed Peas & Kale Soup (page 86) or the Chickpea, Corn, & Spinach Curry (page 82).

The Ground Rules: The 15-minute time includes slicing and dicing, heating, and cooking. It doesn't count the time it takes to grab your ingredients, to give produce a rinse, and to open can(s), if applicable. You should also gather any pots, pans, and equipment you'll need beforehand, like a food processor (for some yummy pestos and hummus varieties).

Tips & Strategies

Here are a few tips and strategies for managing the time from a logistical standpoint, as well as some of my favorite techniques and tricks for achieving lots of flavor in a short amount of time.

Managing the Time: A Simple Exercise in Logistics

Having your ingredients and tools handy: As with many things in life, it helps to set yourself up for success. With 15-minute cooking adventures, there's no exception. Having everything handy goes such a long way when aiming to get your actual cooking time down to a minimum.

Gather all of the ingredients, measuring spoons, and cups. Give the recipe a quick read to know what to expect, and pull out the pans and pots you'll need and any equipment like a food processor, blender, or can opener. Trust me, searching for the can opener or a measuring cup while you're in the middle of a recipe (or while you're getting hangry) is not the end of the world, but it's less than ideal.

Setting up your space efficiently: No matter what your kitchen layout is like, you can set up your station so that speedy cooking will be simple. It is super helpful to set up your cutting board as close as you can to the stove, to cut down on travel time to and from. Being close to the stove will also help you keep an eye on what's cooking in your pan(s). Similarly, have either your trash can or a bowl near your cutting board to throw all your items to be discarded, such as onion peels and zucchini ends.

Making multitasking your best friend: But not multitasking in the overwhelming way, like trying to make dinner while submitting a work presentation and trying to feed your barking puppy at the same time.

Just simple multitasking like this: letting onions cook while you chop a bell pepper before you add it to the pan. Then whisking together a sauce while those cook, and so on. We're basically letting the pan do its thing, cooking the vegetables sequentially and methodically while you work on the next step.

You may be accustomed to cutting all your produce and other ingredients prior to starting any of the cooking. If so, the method used in these recipes will be different. But rest assured, you'll quickly get used to this chop-cook sequential method, and you'll get faster at it the more recipes you try! By the way, when you're making these recipes, if you happen to finish a step sooner than the instructions suggest, you can start preparing the next step.

Using the heat strategically as you go: There's some simple methods you can follow to use the stovetop heat to your advantage. During the cooking process, to avoid burning the food, lower the heat if you need more time to finish prepping the next ingredient. And conversely, you can increase the heat for faster cooking. Your senses will be a great way to keep tabs on how your cooking is going, from the sounds of the ingredients sautéing or bubbling in the pan, to the smell of browning vegetables.

Choosing quicker-cooking noodle shapes: With quick cooking in mind, I've chosen pasta shapes that usually cook to al dente in 9 minutes or less . . . 10 minutes is pushing it but may be possible. This can vary depending on the brand, so just check the package, which will typically tell you the cook time for al dente/firm noodles. However, if you want to use other pasta shapes or brands that are over 9 minutes to al dente, definitely go for it! This book is all about giving you broader options and meal choices to make fast, plant-based cooking more attainable. So that means following your preferences with abandon!

Some examples of relatively quicker-cooking pastas are rice noodles, ramen noodles, soba noodles, angel hair, orzo, rotini, couscous, and penne. On the other hand, spaghetti, ziti, rigatoni, orecchiette, and linguini are some examples that usually take a few more minutes to cook.

While we're on the topic of noodles and pasta (two of my favorite topics of all time), another tip is to use a smaller amount of water in the pot than you may think is needed. If using a large pot, you only need to fill it around 2 inches (5 cm) in depth. Just make sure that you use enough water so that the pasta will be completely submerged as it cooks. This way, you'll save time by not heating way more water than you need.

Knowing your stove/cooker burners: Don't make the devastating mistake (a wee bit dramatic, I know) of putting your pot of water on to boil on the smallest/lowest power burner. It will take much longer to reach a boil, and also longer to reach a boil again once adding your pasta (don't forget to put the lid on your pot for this too!). Also, for a few recipes, we crank the heat up pretty high when cooking our vegetables or tofu. For those, make sure you're using your larger/higher power burners.

Making sure you have a sharp knife: This may seem like a no-brainer, but when we're aiming to cook swiftly (yet safely, of course), you want a properly sharpened knife so that the chopping doesn't take twice as long. I've been there! When using a dull knife, it feels like you're cutting in slow motion. You can typically find a knife sharpener in stores that have a kitchen supply section or online.

Ways to Boost Flavor: My Trusty Arsenal of Tips to Get Crave-Worthy Taste When You're Short on Time

Seasonings: In the same way that multitasking is your best friend, think of those little jars in your spice cabinet or drawer as your teammates. (Just channel your high school swim team, drama club, or debate team. You get the idea.) The herbs and spices will come through to bring bold flavor in a short amount of time, and we use various combinations of these seasonings throughout the recipes in this book. They'll pick up the slack for you when you're too tired or short on time to follow a longer cooking process. Some of my favorites are garlic powder (I use this one a LOT because it's surprising how much flavor it adds, but always feel free to use fresh garlic as desired, keeping in mind that fresh garlic will add time to the prep and cooking steps), dried basil, dried oregano, dried parsley, ground cumin, ground coriander, paprika, chili powder, za'atar seasoning, red chili flakes, and smoked paprika. For soups, I also love tarragon and Italian seasoning blend, which usually includes some thyme and rosemary and/or sage. They add a beautiful depth of flavor in these dishes.

Acidity: Many of these dishes use a lot of lemon and lime, and some use other acids like balsamic vinegar, apple cider vinegar, and rice vinegar. These ingredients go a long way to balance out the overall flavors in the dish and add something special. The vinegars keep well in the pantry, and I like to pick up lemons and limes at the grocery store when I can, as they add a surprising amount of goodness.

Fresh herbs: These are a fantastic way to add flavor in literally the few seconds that it takes to chop them. The payoff is exponential. A tip for using fresh herbs with soft stems (i.e., fresh parsley, dill, cilantro, and basil) is that you can chop the stems along with the leaves. Not the bottom stem area, but the upper parts that hold the majority of the leaves. There's no need to remove each leaf off of the stem for fresh dill, cilantro, and parsley. For pestos that use basil, this works too. If you're using basil leaves that are large, feel free to pick those off of the stems if you prefer. For herbs with tough stems like thyme and rosemary, though, you'll want to pull these leaves off the stem.

If you don't have access to fresh herbs, that's okay. There are enough yummy factors at work in these recipes to still achieve deliciousness, even if you're using the dried herb version. Just note that it's not a 1-to-1 ratio of substituting fresh herbs for its dry counterpart. You can easily look up the substitution ratio online, but a general rule of thumb is to use ⅓ the amount of dried herb as compared to its fresh counterpart. There are a couple of recipes that use variations on pesto, for which the main ingredients are the fresh herbs, so you can substitute store-bought pesto if needed.

Super-flavorful ingredients: Several ingredients that I love to keep in the pantry, when possible, are Dijon mustard, sun-dried tomatoes packed in oil, olives (green and Kalamata), marinated artichoke hearts, capers, roasted red peppers, roasted salted pistachios, pine nuts, sliced or slivered almonds, nutritional yeast, and dried apricot and/or cranberries for touches of sweetness. These ingredients are little powerhouses of flavor and depth, and I use them regularly for a lot of my go-to meals.

Awesome sauces: There are certain ingredients and condiments that allow you to whip up great sauces quickly. For most of the sauces in this cookbook, you'll simply whisk them together in a bowl, or in some cases blend them up in a food processor. These ingredients are helpful to have in your cooking repertoire: vegan mayo and plant-based yogurt, tahini, peanut butter, almond butter, chili garlic sauce, tamari and/or soy sauce, mirin (a type of rice wine that's relatively sweet, used commonly in Japanese cooking), agave nectar and maple syrup (natural sweeteners), and hoisin sauce and gochujang (delicious Asian sauces available in most grocery stores).

Okay! So now that we've covered the inspiration for this book and my favorite tips, let's get cooking!

Savory & Satisfying Pastas

It's no secret that pasta is one of my all-time favorite types of meals, both to eat and to share. It's so nostalgic for me and sticks out as the most anticipated meal of my childhood both on special occasions and regular days. My mom makes her simple yet amazing spaghetti meal for all of the birthdays in our family, and hence, here we are—as an adult, I'm a totally pasta-obsessed lady. From orzo, to penne, to rotini and angel hair . . . and everything in between!

With this chapter, you'll find a multitude of flavors and inspiration from different cuisines. I share pasta dishes that incorporate my favorite shapes and add-ins for this type of meal, while celebrating the fact that we can make awesome pasta meals in 15 minutes. I've also made them very hearty, satisfying, and full of flavor so that you and any omnivore loved ones you share them with won't be missing out. With dishes like Orzo with Cannellini Beans & Artichokes (page 17), we use lots of herbs and citrus as well as super-savory ingredients like olives and toasted pine nuts. And with Sun-Dried Tomato Alfredo Penne with Broccoli (page 30), we mix up the classics with a twist.

Since we're aiming for 15 minutes total time for our meals, we will keep that time element in mind when selecting pastas and cooking method in our recipes here. For example, I'll be making suggestions on pasta shapes and sometimes the pot size and amount of water to use.

I'm certain you'll find some new favorite recipes in this chapter, and I am so excited to share these dishes with you!

Orzo with Cannellini Beans & Artichokes

This dish was inspired by Mediterranean flavors and is brimming with fresh herbs and lemon. It has a light yet really satisfying appeal and is a well-rounded meal with the cannellini beans and zucchini. It also uses one of my favorite pasta shapes! Orzo is really versatile for many types of meals, like soups or room temperature pasta salads, plus it cooks quickly. Here it's served warm with deliciously delicate zucchini, savory and tangy green olives, and flavorful marinated artichokes. Olives and marinated artichokes are great items to keep in the pantry, as they really pack a punch when it comes to flavor; they can also make a quick meal feel more special.

Servings: 3 to 4

8 oz (226 g) orzo

1½ tsp (8 g) kosher salt, divided, plus more to taste

¼ medium red onion

4 tsp (20 ml) olive oil

3 tbsp (24 g) pine nuts

2 medium zucchinis (see Notes)

2 tbsp (6 g) fresh dill, chopped (see Notes)

2 tbsp (6 g) fresh chives, chopped (see Notes)

1 (15-oz [425-g]) can cannellini beans, drained and rinsed

¾ packed cup (126 g) marinated quartered artichoke hearts, drained

½ packed cup (90 g) pitted green olives

1½–2 tbsp (23–30 ml) lemon juice (¾–1 lemon), to taste

1 tsp Dijon mustard

1 tsp Italian seasoning

¾ tsp garlic powder

¼ tsp red chili flakes (optional)

To make the orzo, fill a large pot with around 2 inches (5 cm) of water, cover, and bring to a boil. Add the orzo and 1 teaspoon of salt and cook according to the package directions for al dente, then drain. Meanwhile, preheat a large skillet and a small pot over medium-high heat. Get out a small bowl.

Finely chop the red onion. Add it to the large skillet with the olive oil and the remaining ½ teaspoon of salt. Cook for 5 to 7 minutes, stirring periodically. Meanwhile, toast the pine nuts in the small pot over medium-high heat until lightly golden brown, around 1 minute, stirring every 10 to 20 seconds. Transfer the pine nuts to the bowl to cool.

Trim the ends off the zucchinis. Make zucchini ribbons using a vegetable peeler. Add the zucchinis to the skillet with the onion, gently toss and cook for 2 to 3 minutes until just tender.

Lastly, chop the dill and chives. Add these to the skillet along with the beans, artichoke hearts, olives, lemon juice, mustard, Italian seasoning, garlic powder, and chili flakes, if using, along with the drained orzo. Taste for seasoning and add more salt, if desired.

Notes: This dish is very forgiving with the choice of herbs. Feel free to use those that you have on hand! If using dried herbs in place of any fresh herbs, start in smaller amounts, as dried herbs pack more of a punch.

As an alternative to zucchini ribbons, you may simply slice the trimmed zucchinis lengthwise, then cut into half-moon shapes around ¼ inch (6 mm) thick.

Angel Hair with Lemon, Kale, & Tomatoes

Is it just me, or is there something that's so warm and perfect about angel hair pasta in a flavorful, light sauce with fresh tomatoes, leafy greens, and white beans? Especially when it's topped with vegan feta, crisp panko breadcrumbs, and dill! Once you try this dish, I think you'll agree that this recipe will become a new favorite. It's (of course) quick, and the simple flavors shine with the help of lots of aromatics and a combination of fresh and dried herbs. The toasted breadcrumbs are an optional addition and add a special touch to the dish. But if you want to simplify, feel free to skip them. If you'd like to substitute the plant-based butter, you can replace it with more olive oil or some additional vegetable broth.

Servings: 4

3 tsp (15 g) kosher salt, divided

8 oz (226 g) angel hair pasta

⅓ cup (18 g) panko breadcrumbs (optional)

1 large shallot

2 tbsp (30 ml) olive oil

½ tsp black pepper

3 large cloves garlic

1 pint (298 g) cherry or grape tomatoes

1 cup (240 ml) vegetable broth

1 tbsp (5 g) dried basil

3 large kale leaves

1 (15-oz [425-g]) can cannellini beans, drained and rinsed

2–3 tbsp (7–10 g) fresh dill, to taste (see Note)

3 tbsp (45 ml) lemon juice (about 1½ lemons)

½ cup (75 g) crumbled plant-based feta (optional)

1 tbsp (14 g) plant-based butter (optional)

Fill a large pot with around 2 inches (5 cm) of water, enough to fully submerge the pasta, cover, and bring to a boil. Then add 2 teaspoons (10 g) of salt and the angel hair pasta, stir, and cover to bring to a boil again. Uncover and cook until just al dente, according to the package directions, then drain.

Meanwhile, over medium heat, preheat a large pan or skillet, as well as a small saucepan for the breadcrumbs, if using. Add the breadcrumbs to the small saucepan and toast them for 1 to 3 minutes, stirring occasionally, or until they're lightly golden brown. Then transfer them to a plate or bowl to cool.

While those are toasting, finely chop the shallot and add it to the large pan, along with the olive oil, remaining 1 teaspoon of salt, and pepper. Stir and let it cook while you mince the garlic. Add the garlic, and let it cook while you halve the tomatoes. Add the tomatoes to the pan, along with the vegetable broth and dried basil. Stir the broth and simmer while you prepare the kale.

De-stem and thinly slice the kale, then add it to the pan along with the cannellini beans. Stir and cook for 1 minute while you finely chop the dill. Add the dill, lemon juice, and optional feta and plant-based butter to the pan. Stir and serve, topping with the toasted panko breadcrumbs, if using.

Note: If you're out of fresh dill, use around ½ teaspoon of dried dill if you have it. Feel free to drizzle in another tablespoon (15 ml) of olive oil just prior to serving.

Sun-Dried Tomato & Roasted Pepper Ricotta Pasta

This delicious Sun-Dried Tomato & Roasted Pepper Ricotta Pasta is a twist on a dish that I used to have a lot growing up at home and at gatherings with extended family, which was a penne or ziti pasta with red sauce and ricotta cheese. For this vegan version, we make a savory and flavorful "ricotta" from tofu, seasonings, sun-dried tomatoes, and roasted red peppers. It creates a dreamy and creamy ricotta that is combined with a homemade marinara sauce for the pasta. The baby spinach adds some green, because that's always welcome. You can serve this meal alongside vegetables or a big salad. Time tip: While the sauce is cooking, start adding the ricotta ingredients into the food processor. The recipe makes more tofu ricotta than the amount you'll need for the pasta sauce, so you can use the extra ricotta as a delicious topping for toast and flatbreads or as a dip for pita or tortilla chips.

Servings: 4

8 oz (226 g) penne pasta

3¾ tsp (23 g) kosher salt, divided

1 small yellow onion

3 tbsp (45 ml) olive oil

1½ tsp (3 g) black pepper, divided

2 cloves garlic

1 (28-oz [784-g]) can crushed tomatoes

½ tsp dried oregano

2 cups (60 g) baby spinach

14 oz (396 g) extra-firm tofu

1½ tbsp (23 ml) lemon juice (about ¾ lemon)

1 tsp dried basil

¼ tsp onion powder

¾ tsp garlic powder

½ cup (114 g) sun-dried tomatoes packed in oil, drained

¼ cup (80 g) roasted red peppers, drained

Red chili flakes, for serving (optional)

Vegan Parmesan, for serving (optional)

To make the penne, fill a large pot with 2 inches (5 cm) of water, enough to fully submerge the pasta, cover, and bring to a boil. Once boiling, add the penne and 2 teaspoons (10 g) of salt, stir, and cover to bring to a boil. Then uncover and boil until al dente, according to the package directions. Drain the penne.

Meanwhile, preheat a medium saucepan on medium heat. Finely chop the yellow onion and add it to the pan with the olive oil, 1 teaspoon of salt, and ½ teaspoon of pepper. Stir and cook for 1 to 2 minutes. While the onion is cooking, mince the garlic and add it to the pan, then cook for 3 to 4 minutes. Add the crushed tomatoes and dried oregano, and cook at a gentle simmer, partially covered, for 3 to 4 minutes. Add the baby spinach to the sauce during the last minute of cooking, stirring to let it wilt into the sauce.

To prepare the ricotta, gently squeeze the tofu over the sink with your hands to remove the excess water. Add the tofu to a food processor, along with the remaining ¾ teaspoon of salt and 1 teaspoon of pepper, lemon juice, dried basil, onion powder, garlic powder, sun-dried tomatoes, and roasted peppers. Blend well, scraping down the sides as needed. Add ¾ to 1 cup (180 to 240 ml) of the ricotta to the sauce and swirl it in. Add the sauce to the drained pasta, top with red chili flakes and vegan parmesan to taste, if using, and serve with extra ricotta as desired.

Veggie Pasta with Lemon Cream Sauce & Toasted Breadcrumbs

This recipe is a spin on a recipe for pasta with cashew cream sauce from my blog. It's rich and decadent but with a sauce made primarily of cashews, vegetable broth, and seasonings rather than traditional dairy cream sauce ingredients. For convenience that still tastes awesome, we use a frozen vegetable mix of corn, peas, and cut green beans. This mix is so great in here when combined with the red onion and creamy sauce. You can adjust the amount of lemon juice to your preference, and feel free to add more than the recipe calls for. To thin the sauce, add another ¼ cup (60 ml) of the vegetable broth, if desired. Tip to warm any leftovers: Add some vegetable broth during heating, as the sauce gets thicker as it cools.

Servings: 4 to 6

12 oz (336 g) penne pasta
3¼ tsp (17 g) kosher salt, divided
2 cups (292 g) raw cashews
¼ cup (14 g) panko breadcrumbs
½ large red onion
1 tbsp (15 ml) olive oil
2½ cups (319 g) frozen vegetable mix
2 cups (480 ml) vegetable broth
1 tsp Dijon mustard
1 tsp black pepper
2 tsp (3 g) nutritional yeast
3 tbsp (45 ml) lemon juice (about 1½ lemons)
1½ tsp (4 g) garlic powder
½ tsp paprika
1 tsp dried oregano
1 tsp dried basil
Dash of cayenne pepper

To make the pasta, fill a large pot with 2 inches (5 cm) of water, enough to fully submerge the pasta, cover, and bring to a boil. Once boiling, add the pasta and 2 teaspoons (10 g) of salt. Stir and cook until al dente, according to the package directions. Before draining the pasta, scoop out and reserve around ½ cup (120 ml) of the pasta cooking water. Drain the penne.

Meanwhile, add the cashews to a small saucepan with enough fresh water to cover them. Bring it to a boil, covered, and cook for 5 to 6 minutes, then drain.

To toast the breadcrumbs, while the cashews and pasta are cooking, add the breadcrumbs to a small saucepan or skillet and cook on medium-high heat for 2 to 4 minutes, stirring often, until they are lightly golden brown. Set them aside for topping the pasta later.

Preheat a large pan on medium heat. Finely chop the red onion and add it to the pan with the olive oil, stir, and let the onion cook for 3 to 4 minutes, stirring periodically. Add the frozen mixed vegetables, stir, and cook for 3 to 4 minutes.

Warm the broth in a bowl in the microwave for 60 seconds. To a blender, add the warm vegetable broth, mustard, remaining 1¼ teaspoons (7 g) of salt, pepper, nutritional yeast, lemon juice, garlic powder, paprika, dried oregano, and dried basil. Add the cashews and blend until smooth. Add the cooked pasta and the cashew sauce to the pan with the vegetables, stir, then stir in the pasta cooking water to thin the sauce, if desired. Serve and top with the toasted breadcrumbs and a dash of cayenne pepper for spicy heat.

Penne with Peas, Vegan Sausage, & Marinara

Sometimes you just want a simple and absolutely delicious pasta meal with red sauce. Or if you're like me, you could eat it most days of the week. It's comforting, super simple, and downright tasty. It's also quite nostalgic for me, as my mom used to make a similar pasta with ground beef. This recipe uses vegan sausage, but you can also use vegan ground beef substitute. Alternatively, you can skip the meat replacement and use chopped, sautéed mushrooms or lentils. Just season them well with salt, pepper, and garlic powder. This Penne with Peas, Vegan Sausage, & Marinara will be great on its own, or you can top it with vegan Parmesan and serve with crusty bread.

Servings: 4

16 oz (454 g) penne pasta

¼ large red onion

2 tbsp (30 ml) olive oil

1 tsp kosher salt

½ tsp black pepper

4 vegan sausages (about 3.5 oz [98 g] total), thawed if frozen (I like Beyond Meat® Beyond Sausage® Plant-Based Links and Field Roast® Plant-Based Sausages)

½ tsp garlic powder

½ tsp dried basil, plus extra for garnish

½ tsp dried oregano

2 large cloves garlic

1½ cups (151 g) frozen peas

1 (28-oz [784-g]) can crushed tomatoes

Grated vegan Parmesan, for serving

Crusty bread, for serving

Fill a large pot with 2 inches (5 cm) of water, enough to fully submerge the pasta, cover, and bring to a boil. Add the penne and cook according to the package directions for al dente. Before draining the pasta, scoop out and reserve ½ cup (120 ml) of the pasta cooking water. Drain the pasta.

Meanwhile, preheat a large pan over medium heat and finely chop the red onion. Add it to the pan with the olive oil, salt, and pepper. Stir and let the onion cook for 1 to 2 minutes while preparing the vegan sausages.

Slice the vegan sausages crosswise, around ½ inch (1.3 cm) thick, then add them to the pan along with the garlic powder, dried basil, and dried oregano. Let the sausages cook for 3 to 4 minutes. During this time, mince the garlic. Add the garlic and peas to the pan, gently stir, and cook for 3 to 4 minutes. Lastly, add the crushed tomatoes and up to ½ cup (120 ml) of the pasta cooking water to thin the sauce to your preference. Stir and cook for 1 to 2 minutes. Serve the pasta with the sauce, grated vegan Parmesan, and crusty bread. Sprinkle with extra dried basil to garnish, if desired.

Creamy Mediterranean-Inspired Pasta Salad

This creamy pasta salad is a twist on the typical version that was often served at outdoor gatherings and cookouts growing up. It's super savory, with a really flavorful yogurt and mayo–based dressing and lots of my favorite ingredients like sun-dried tomatoes, marinated artichoke hearts, and roasted red peppers. The chickpeas make this extra satisfying for a full meal, and the tomatoes add a pop of freshness. I love the combination of fresh dill and fresh basil, and this creamy pasta salad uses both. When I make this pasta, I find it really hard to have just one helping. Thankfully, it's quick to whip up if you run out sooner than expected!

Servings: 4

8 oz (226 g) penne pasta

2½ tsp (13 g) kosher salt, divided, plus more to taste

1 tsp black pepper

1 tsp garlic powder

1 tbsp (15 ml) apple cider vinegar

2 tbsp (30 ml) lemon juice (about 1 lemon)

2 tsp (10 ml) Dijon mustard

2 tbsp (30 ml) plain, unsweetened almond-based yogurt (see Notes)

2 tbsp (30 ml) vegan mayo

1 cup (149 g) cherry or grape tomatoes

2 tbsp (7 g) fresh dill (see Notes)

2 tbsp (20 g) finely chopped red onion (optional)

⅓ cup (107 g) sliced roasted red peppers, drained

½ cup (114 g) sliced sun-dried tomatoes packed in oil, drained

¾ cup (126 g) quartered marinated artichoke hearts, drained

1 cup (164 g) canned chickpeas, drained and rinsed

4–6 fresh basil leaves (optional, see Notes)

Fill a large pot with 2 inches (5 cm) of water, enough to fully submerge the pasta, cover, and bring to a boil. Add the penne and 2 teaspoons (10 g) of salt, stir, and cook to al dente, according to the package directions. Drain and rinse the pasta in cool water before adding it into the rest of the ingredients at the end.

Meanwhile, prepare the dressing. To a large mixing bowl, add the remaining ½ teaspoon of salt, pepper, garlic powder, apple cider vinegar, lemon juice, mustard, almond-based yogurt, and vegan mayo, and then stir together.

Halve the tomatoes and finely chop the fresh dill. Add the tomatoes, dill, red onion, if using, roasted red peppers, sun-dried tomatoes, artichoke hearts, and chickpeas to the mixing bowl. Thinly slice the fresh basil leaves for garnishing the pasta salad, if using. Add the cooked pasta to the bowl, and gently toss everything together. Taste and add more salt, if desired. Top the salad with the fresh basil and serve.

Notes: This pasta salad works well with almond-based yogurt given its neutral flavor, or plain soy-based yogurt works well also. Coconut yogurt tends to have a sweeter flavor, so I wouldn't recommend it for this.

You may substitute 2 teaspoons (2 g) of dried dill for the fresh dill, and ½ teaspoon of dried basil for the fresh basil leaves.

Peanut Sauce Noodles with Shredded Sprouts & Edamame

These creamy and nutty noodles are the perfect light dinner that combines some of my favorite things. It doesn't get much better than noodles in a rich, Asian-inspired peanut sauce! We combine the noodles with some super-nutritious vegetables as well—Brussels sprouts and red cabbage—that result in a beautifully colorful dish. The shredded sprouts become bright green in the pan, and the red cabbage turns that beautiful purple. Adding in edamame gives us some great texture, plus it rounds out the meal with plant-based protein. We use rice noodles here, but this dish would also be amazing with pure buckwheat noodles, ramen noodles, or vermicelli. You can buy presliced Brussels sprouts to save some time too!

Servings: 3

8 oz (226 g) rice noodles

⅔ cup (82 g) frozen shelled edamame

¼ lb (113 g) Brussels sprouts

2 tsp (10 ml) toasted sesame oil

1½ cups (105 g) thinly sliced red cabbage

½ tsp onion powder

6 tbsp (96 g) natural peanut butter (see Note)

1 tsp garlic powder

2 tsp (10 g) ginger paste

2 tbsp (30 ml) agave nectar

2 tbsp (30 ml) chili garlic sauce

2 tbsp (30 ml) reduced-sodium soy sauce

2 tbsp (30 ml) lime juice (1–1½ limes)

2 tbsp (30 ml) water, divided

2 tbsp (2 g) cilantro

2 tsp (6 g) sesame seeds, for serving

Fill a large pot with around 2 inches (5 cm) of water, enough to fully submerge the noodles, cover, and bring to a boil. Right when the water boils, add the noodles, stir, and cover to bring it to a boil again. Then uncover and cook the noodles according to the package directions for al dente. Drain them and rinse well under warm, running water.

Place the edamame in a small bowl and cover with warm water to thaw.

Meanwhile, preheat a large skillet on medium heat. Cut the Brussels sprouts in half lengthwise through the stem, then "shred" them by thinly slicing crosswise. Add the Brussels sprouts and toasted sesame oil to the pan, stir, and let it cook for 1 to 2 minutes. Add the red cabbage and onion powder to the pan, stir, and cook for 2 to 3 minutes, stirring periodically. Drain the edamame. Remove the pan from the heat, then pour in the edamame.

To make the sauce, add the peanut butter, garlic powder, ginger paste, agave nectar, chili garlic sauce, soy sauce, lime juice, and 1 tablespoon (15 ml) of water to a bowl, and whisk together. If the sauce seems too thick, add another tablespoon (15 ml) of water. Finely chop the fresh cilantro and add it to the skillet, along with the noodles and sauce. Gently toss everything together and top with the sesame seeds.

Note: For this recipe, use the natural or runny kind of peanut butter, where the oil separates from the peanuts in the jar. This type blends easily with the other ingredients using a whisk. If you don't have it, you may need to use a blender to get the sauce nice and creamy.

Sun-Dried Tomato Alfredo Penne with Broccoli

There's something so comforting about a bowl or plate of pasta with a creamy sauce, and tons of bonus points if there's broccoli too. Broccoli is just so perfect for pastas, and I'm addicted to that combination, especially creamy pasta. But rather than continue the diatribe about how much I love these things, I'll keep it short and sweet and say that this one is a cozy keeper. The sun-dried tomatoes add great depth in a savory and slightly sweet way. There's a combination of vegan cheeses in this recipe, but you can feel free to use either cheddar or mozzarella if you only have one of them on hand. The fresh parsley and red chili flakes top this off perfectly, and you can add as much of those as your heart desires.

Servings: 4

8 oz (226 g) penne pasta

3 cups (273 g) broccoli florets, cut small

¾ cups (180 ml) water

2 tbsp (28 g) plant-based butter

2 tbsp (16 g) flour

2 cups (480 g) plain, unsweetened oat milk

½ cup (120 ml) full-fat coconut milk, canned

1¼ tsp (7 g) kosher salt

1 tsp black pepper

1½ tsp (4 g) garlic powder

¾ tsp onion powder

¼ cup (28 g) plant-based shredded cheddar

¼ cup (28 g) plant-based shredded mozzarella

1 tsp Dijon mustard

2 tbsp (10 g) nutritional yeast

1 tbsp (4 g) fresh parsley

¼ cup (57 g) sliced sun-dried tomatoes packed in oil, drained

Red chili flakes, for serving

To make the pasta, fill a large pot with 2 inches (5 cm) of water, enough to fully submerge the pasta, cover, and bring to a boil. Once it's boiling, add the pasta, cover, and bring to a boil again. Once it's boiling, you can remove the lid and continue to cook until al dente, according to the package directions. Drain the pasta.

Cook the broccoli florets by adding them to a large pan along with the water, then cover and bring to a boil. Reduce the heat and let the broccoli cook until it's bright green and fork tender, 8 to 10 minutes depending on the size. Drain away any remaining water.

Meanwhile, prepare the sauce. Place a medium-sized saucepan over medium heat and add the butter. When the butter melts, add the flour and whisk until combined. Then slowly drizzle in the oat milk, whisking constantly as you pour. Add the coconut milk, salt, pepper, garlic powder, and onion powder. Stir and let the sauce continue to cook for 1 to 2 minutes to reach a simmer, then stir in the plant-based cheddar and mozzarella. Let the sauce cook for 1 to 2 minutes as the cheese melts, then whisk in the mustard and nutritional yeast.

Finely chop the fresh parsley. Combine the cooked pasta with the sauce, sun-dried tomatoes, broccoli, and fresh parsley. Serve topped with red chili flakes.

Creamy Carrot, Zucchini, & Olive Pasta

This veggie-filled pasta is loaded up with the finer things in life—that is, lots of veggies. There are onions, carrots, tomatoes, and zucchini. And if that's not enough to woo you, this pasta also has a light, creamy sauce along with fresh parsley and Kalamata olives. The combination is dreamy, and you may find yourself eating straight from the pan! Make sure to use your favorite marinara sauce if using store-bought, or you can use the marinara recipe from the Sun-Dried Tomato & Roasted Pepper Ricotta Pasta (page 21).

Servings: 4

8 oz (226 g) penne pasta

3 tsp (15 g) kosher salt, divided

½ small red onion

2 tbsp (30 ml) olive oil

1 large carrot

1 medium zucchini

½ cup (75 g) cherry or grape tomatoes

¾ cup (123 g) canned chickpeas

1½ tsp (4 g) garlic powder

1½ tsp (3 g) dried basil

1 cup (240 ml) marinara sauce

½ cup (120 ml) full-fat coconut milk, canned

1 tbsp (4 g) fresh parsley (see Note)

12 pitted Kalamata olives (optional)

Red chili flakes or black pepper, for serving (optional)

To make the penne, fill a large pot with 2 inches (5 cm) of water, enough to fully submerge the pasta, cover, and bring to a boil. Once boiling, add the penne and 2 teaspoons (10 g) of salt, stir, and cover to bring it to a boil again. Remove the lid and continue to cook until al dente, according to the package directions, then drain.

Meanwhile, preheat a large pan on medium-high heat and finely chop the onion. Add it to the pan with the olive oil and remaining 1 teaspoon of salt. Stir and let the onion cook for 1 to 2 minutes while preparing the carrot. Peel the carrot, trim off the ends, cut it down the middle lengthwise, then make thin slices crosswise. Add the carrot to the pan and stir, reducing the heat to medium. Let the carrot cook, covered, for 3 to 4 minutes.

While the carrots are cooking, cut the zucchini in a small dice and add it to the pan. Stir the vegetables and let them cook for 1 minute. Slice the cherry tomatoes in half and add them to the pan. Some browning is good and adds flavor to the vegetables.

Drain and rinse the chickpeas. To the pan with the veggies, stir in the garlic powder, dried basil, marinara sauce, coconut milk, and chickpeas, and let it gently simmer, uncovered, for 1 to 2 minutes, or until the zucchini is fork tender. While the sauce is simmering, chop the fresh parsley. You can coarsely chop the olives, if using, or leave them whole. Stir the parsley, olives, and cooked pasta into the sauce, and serve with red chili flakes for spicy heat or black pepper, if desired.

Note: This recipe works perfectly well if you want to substitute dried parsley; use ½ teaspoon.

Roasted Red Pepper Chipotle Pasta Salad

This Roasted Red Pepper Chipotle Pasta Salad is filled with tomatoes, cucumber, corn, and avocado, and is topped with cilantro and scallions for extra flair. It has a creamy and tangy dressing that's flavored with roasted red peppers and chipotle in adobo. The creaminess comes from a combination of vegan mayo and yogurt. It's a perfect colorful pasta that's delicious at room temperature or chilled. I find that almond-based and soy-based yogurt works well for this, where a coconut-based yogurt may be too much on the sweet side. You can use your favorite plant-based yogurt, though, as there are many options to love. This colorful and flavorful pasta salad would be perfect for a summer picnic or light meal.

Servings: 4

Pasta Salad
8 oz (226 g) rotini pasta
½ tbsp (8 ml) avocado oil
2 cups (272 g) frozen corn
Pinch of kosher salt and black pepper
1 cup (149 g) cherry or grape tomatoes
½ cup (160 g) roasted red peppers, drained well
½ seedless cucumber
1 avocado
2 tbsp (2 g) cilantro
2 tbsp (20 g) thinly sliced red onion (optional)
2 tbsp (6 g) sliced scallions, for serving (optional)

Dressing
¼ cup (60 ml) vegan mayo
¼ cup (60 ml) plain, unsweetened almond-based yogurt
⅓ cup (107 g) roasted red peppers, drained well
1 tsp sauce from a can of chipotles in adobo (see Note)
½ tbsp (8 ml) lime juice (¼–½ lime)

1 tsp kosher salt
½ tsp black pepper
1¼ tsp (4 g) garlic powder
½ tsp ground cumin
1 tsp dried parsley

To prepare the pasta, fill a large pot with 2 inches (5 cm) of water, enough to fully submerge the pasta, cover, and bring to a boil. Add the rotini, stir, and cover to bring back to a boil. Remove the lid and cook to al dente, according to the package directions. Drain and rinse the pasta in cool water.

Place a large pan over medium-high heat. Add the avocado oil and frozen corn to the pan and season the corn with a pinch of salt and pepper. Let these cook for 4 to 5 minutes, stirring occasionally, until lightly browned. Transfer the corn to a large mixing bowl to cool.

Meanwhile, halve the tomatoes, chop the roasted red peppers, dice the cucumber and avocado, and finely chop the cilantro. Add these into the mixing bowl, along with the red onion, if using.

For the dressing, to a food processor or blender, add the mayo, yogurt, red peppers, adobo sauce, lime juice, salt, pepper, garlic powder, cumin, and parsley, and blend until smooth. Add the dressing and cooked pasta into the mixing bowl, and gently stir to incorporate the dressing. Top the salad with the sliced scallions, if using.

Note: To kick up the spice level, go ahead and add one of the canned chipotle peppers, finely chopped, in addition to the teaspoon of sauce.

Creamy "Beefy" Rotini with Mushrooms & Spinach

Are you ready for a warm and cozy hug in a bowl? This rotini pasta has savory, "beefy" goodness and the classically comforting combination of mushrooms and spinach. The savory factor is boosted even further with vegan cream cheese, lots of dried herbs, and marinated artichokes. Artichokes may be an unexpected ingredient in a pasta like this, but I think you'll be very pleasantly surprised with what it brings to the dish. Plus, it's such a simple dish to make! While the pasta is cooking, the rest of the meal comes together easily in one pan. Perfect for an easy yet delicious weeknight meal, I think this rotini will be a new favorite recipe in your rotation!

Servings: 3 to 4

8 oz (226 g) rotini pasta

2 tsp (10 g) kosher salt, divided

1 shallot

2 tsp (10 ml) olive oil

12 oz (336 g) ground meat substitute, thawed if frozen (I like Beyond Meat and Impossible Foods™ ground burger)

8 oz (226 g) cremini or baby portobello mushrooms

⅓ cup (80 ml) white wine (see Note)

2 tsp (6 g) garlic powder

1 tsp dried tarragon

1½ tsp (2 g) Italian seasoning

½ tsp black pepper

½ cup (120 ml) vegetable broth

½ cup (116 g) vegan cream cheese

¾ cup (126 g) chopped marinated artichoke hearts, drained

2½ tbsp (40 g) tomato paste

2 tsp (3 g) nutritional yeast

1½ packed cups (45 g) baby spinach

Red chili flakes, for serving

Fill a large pot with around 2 inches (5 cm) of water, enough to fully submerge the pasta, cover, and bring to a boil. Then add 2 teaspoons (10 g) of salt and the rotini, stir, and cover to bring to a boil. Then uncover and cook until just al dente, according to the package directions. Before draining the pasta, scoop out and reserve around ½ cup (120 ml) of the pasta cooking water.

Meanwhile, preheat a large pan over medium-high heat. Finely chop the shallot and add it to the pan along with the olive oil and ground meat substitute. Stir and cook while you prepare the mushrooms. Slice the mushrooms and add them to the pan. Cook for 6 to 7 minutes, stirring periodically.

Add the white wine, garlic powder, dried tarragon, and Italian seasoning, allowing the liquid to bubble for 1 to 2 minutes as the spices are going in. Add in the pepper, broth, cream cheese, artichoke hearts, tomato paste, nutritional yeast, spinach, and the cooked pasta. Stir well, and add in some of the pasta cooking water, if desired, to thin. Then top it with red chili flakes for some spicy heat and garnish with extra dried tarragon, if desired.

Note: If needed, a great substitute for the white wine would be to use extra vegetable broth and a squeeze of lemon juice.

Green Goddess Angel Hair Pasta

This green goddess angel hair recipe combines lots of favorites, with a super-savory pesto and twirlable pasta coziness. Mushrooms, zucchini, and peas come together as the veggies for this pasta. I have to say, they make up a pretty irresistible veggie team in this recipe. It's a great balance of savory from the mushrooms and lighter vibes from the zucchini, peas, and fresh herbs. I prefer grated vegan Parmesan in this recipe. If you use shreds, you may need a bit more than the recipe calls for. Also, if you choose to use a natural vegan Parmesan—for example, one made from ground cashews and nutritional yeast—start with the smaller amount, taste, and add more if you like. The pine nuts make an important addition, too, to provide earthy nuttiness and body to the pesto. Lots of lemon is welcome in this dish, so please feel free to increase the amount, and enjoy!

Servings: 4

8 oz (226 g) angel hair pasta

6 oz (170 g) mushrooms

¼ cup + 1 tsp (65 ml) olive oil, divided

1 large zucchini

1 cup (134 g) frozen peas

1 tsp garlic powder

1 tsp kosher salt

1 tsp black pepper

1 medium bunch fresh basil leaves

1 packed tbsp (4 g) fresh parsley

1 tbsp (15 ml) lemon juice (about ½ lemon)

¼ cup (34 g) pine nuts, plus more for serving

2–3 tbsp (30–45 g) grated vegan Parmesan, plus more to taste (I like the Go Veggie® grated Parmesan-style topping)

⅓ cup (59 g) Kalamata olives

To make the angel hair, fill a large pot with around 2 inches (5 cm) of water, enough to fully submerge the noodles, cover, and bring to a boil. Right when the water boils, add the pasta, stir, and cover to bring the water to a boil again. Then uncover and cook the angel hair according to package directions until al dente. Before draining the noodles, scoop out and reserve around ¼ cup (60 ml) of the pasta cooking water. Drain the noodles.

Meanwhile, preheat a large pan on medium-high heat. Thinly slice the mushrooms and add them to the pan with 1 tablespoon plus 1 teaspoon (20 ml) of the olive oil. Stir and let them cook for 4 to 5 minutes, stirring occasionally. While the mushrooms are cooking, trim the ends off the zucchini, dice it, and add it to the pan. Stir, and let these cook for 2 to 3 minutes. Stir in the frozen peas, garlic powder, salt, and pepper. Let the vegetables continue to cook for 3 to 4 minutes, stirring periodically. Some browning is fine.

While the vegetables are cooking, prepare the pesto. To a food processor, add the fresh basil leaves (some stem is fine), remaining 3 tablespoons (45 ml) of olive oil, parsley, lemon juice, pine nuts, and vegan Parmesan. Blend the pesto, scraping down the sides as needed. Add the Kalamata olives, pesto, and cooked pasta to the vegetables, and gently stir. Stir in some of the pasta cooking water, if desired, to help coat the pasta evenly with the pesto. Top with the remaining pine nuts (and some more vegan Parmesan if you like!).

Lemon & Mushroom Orzo with Kale & Sun-Dried Tomatoes

When I think about this recipe, the song "My Favorite Things" from The Sound of Music *comes to mind. It includes a lot of my favorite ingredients, which may not be too surprising if you've been following my recipes for a while. This includes lemon, orzo, mushrooms, fresh tomatoes, and hints of Dijon mustard with sun-dried tomatoes. This dish will make a great meal prep. Just serve leftovers with some extra lemon juice and/ or olive oil, since the dressing gets somewhat absorbed in the fridge overnight. Feel free to add fresh herbs to your heart's content as well. Some great options would be fresh basil, parsley, or thyme.*

Servings: 3 to 4

8 oz (226 g) orzo pasta

2 tsp (10 g) kosher salt, divided

3 tbsp (45 ml) olive oil

8 oz (226 g) presliced mushrooms

2 cloves garlic, minced

1½ cups (225 g) cherry or grape tomatoes

1 tsp black pepper

1 tsp garlic powder

¼ cup (60 ml) dry white wine

2 medium kale leaves

2 tsp (1 g) dried parsley

⅓ cup (76 g) julienned sun-dried tomatoes packed in oil, drained

¼ cup (60 ml) lemon juice (about 2 lemons)

2 tsp (10 ml) Dijon mustard

1–2 tsp (2–3 g) nutritional yeast, to taste

¼ cup (31 g) coarsely chopped roasted pistachios (optional)

To make the orzo, fill a large pot with 2 inches (5 cm) of water, enough to fully submerge the pasta, cover, and bring to a boil. Add the orzo and 1 teaspoon of salt, and cook according to the package directions for al dente, then drain the orzo.

Meanwhile, preheat a large pan on medium-high heat. Add the olive oil and mushrooms, and cook for 5 to 6 minutes, stirring periodically, until the mushrooms start to brown.

Meanwhile, mince the garlic and halve the cherry tomatoes. Add the garlic, remaining 1 teaspoon of salt, pepper, and garlic powder to the pan, and reduce the heat to medium. Stir and carefully add the white wine and cherry tomatoes. Let the wine gently bubble away for 1 to 2 minutes until about half the liquid is remaining. While the wine is simmering, chop the kale into small bite-sized pieces, removing any tough stems.

Add the kale, dried parsley, sun-dried tomatoes, lemon juice, mustard, and nutritional yeast. Stir and cook for 1 minute to wilt the kale, then add the cooked orzo. Stir and serve it topped with the chopped pistachios, if desired.

Angel Hair with Chickpeas, Broccolini, & Peas

This Angel Hair with Chickpeas, Broccolini, & Peas is light, lemony, and filled with garlicky goodness. For me, this pasta is really filling, too, thanks to the chickpeas and peas. The broccolini gets buttery and tender in the best way, and it is such a great pairing with the tangy and sweet roasted red peppers. You can substitute broccoli florets if you don't have broccolini. You'll never see me upset at adding broccoli to pasta. It's just so good either way!

Servings: 3 to 4

8 oz (226 g) angel hair pasta

3 tsp (15 g) kosher salt, divided

2 bunches broccolini

3 tbsp (45 ml) olive oil

½ cup (120 ml) vegetable broth

½ cup (160 g) roasted red peppers, drained

2 tbsp (17 g) minced garlic

1 tbsp (14 g) plant-based butter or olive oil

1 (15-oz [425-g]) can chickpeas, drained and rinsed

½ cup (67 g) frozen peas

½ tsp black pepper

2 tsp (2 g) Italian seasoning blend

1 tsp garlic powder

¼ cup (28 g) shredded vegan Parmesan (see Note)

2 tbsp (18 g) capers, drained

1 tbsp (15 ml) lemon juice (about ½ lemon), plus more for serving

Red chili flakes, for serving

To make the pasta, fill a large pot with 2 inches (5 cm) of water, enough to fully submerge the pasta, cover, and bring to a boil. Once it's boiling, add the pasta and 2 teaspoons (10 g) of salt, stir, and cover to bring to a boil again. Remove the cover and continue to boil until al dente, according to the package directions. Before draining the pasta, scoop out and reserve around ¼ cup (60 ml) of the pasta cooking water. Drain the pasta.

Meanwhile, preheat a large pan on medium heat. Trim the bottom from the broccolini so that you're left with the florets and a bit of stem. Cut the florets into bite-sized pieces. Add these to the pan with the olive oil and vegetable broth. Stir, cover, and let it cook for 2 to 3 minutes.

While the broccolini is cooking, coarsely chop the roasted red peppers. Add the garlic, roasted red peppers, butter, chickpeas, peas, remaining 1 teaspoon of salt, pepper, Italian seasoning, and garlic powder to the pan. Stir the vegetables and continue to cook partially covered for 2 to 4 minutes, or until the broccolini is tender.

Add the ¼ cup (60 ml) of pasta cooking water to the pan with the veggies, along with the vegan Parmesan, capers, and lemon juice, as well as the cooked pasta. Toss everything to combine and add more lemon juice or pasta cooking water, if desired. Serve with red chili flakes for some spicy heat.

Note: The vegan Parmesan can be substituted with nutritional yeast, but start small with 1 tablespoon (5 g), given its robust flavor.

Lighter Side:
Quesadillas, Tacos, Sandwiches, Flatbreads, & Salads

To say I'm in love with this chapter would be an understatement. Perhaps "food soul mates" is a more appropriate term for it. Combined in this chapter is a mix of all the good things. There's something for everyone to love, and these recipes are equally enjoyable no matter what season it is. They all feel right for either dinner or lunch, which perhaps is the reason I love them so much—they are there for you, all day long!

It's hard to pick out my favorite recipes from this chapter, and I hope that you'll feel the same once you try them. Many of these recipes have become family favorites, like the Spicy & Cheesy Chickpea & Mushroom Flatbread (page 68) and the Warm Lentil & Carrot Salad with Herbs & Balsamic Vinaigrette (page 75). I'm obsessed with the Chickpea Tempeh Salad Open-Faced Sandwich (page 56) and find it hard not to eat the whole mixture straight from the mixing bowl. But these are just some examples. As the chapter title states, there's everything from tacos to salads to sandwiches.

Spiced Chickpea & Kale Salad with Vegan Honey Mustard

I'm so excited to share this recipe, as it is a testament to how yummy a kale salad can be. The vegan honey mustard is so simple and incredibly yummy, and it's great in a variety of salads or as a dipping sauce. With seasoned chickpeas, crisp cucumber, tangy olives, and crunchy almonds, I think this salad will become a favorite for you too.

Servings: 3 to 4

Salad
1 (15-oz [425-g]) can chickpeas
1 tsp avocado oil
¼ tsp kosher salt
¼ tsp garlic powder
½ tsp paprika
Dash of cayenne pepper
1 medium bundle kale
Juice of ¼ lemon
1 tsp olive oil
½ medium seedless cucumber
1⅓ cups (200 g) cherry or grape tomatoes
⅓ cup (59 g) Kalamata olives
⅓ cup (36 g) sliced almonds

Dressing
¼ cup (60 ml) vegan mayo
4 tsp (20 ml) Dijon mustard
2 tbsp (30 ml) agave nectar
¼ tsp kosher salt
¼ tsp garlic powder

To make the chickpeas, preheat a pan on medium heat. Drain and rinse the chickpeas. Add the chickpeas, avocado oil, salt, garlic powder, paprika, and cayenne. Stir the chickpeas and cook them for 2 to 3 minutes, until they are very lightly crisp, stirring periodically.

Set out a large mixing or serving bowl. While the chickpeas are cooking, prepare the kale. Wash and pat the leaves dry, then cut out the tough stems. Cut the leaves into small bite-sized pieces and add them to the bowl. Add the lemon juice and olive oil, and gently massage the leaves to soften them.

Then dice the cucumber and halve the cherry tomatoes. Coarsely chop the Kalamata olives, or you can leave them whole.

For the dressing, to a small bowl, add the mayo, mustard, agave nectar, salt, and garlic powder, and whisk them together.

To assemble the salad, top the kale with the chickpeas, cucumber, tomatoes, olives, and almonds. Drizzle the dressing over the salad.

Easy Ramen Noodles with Red Cabbage & Mushrooms

These are my favorite super-quick noodles, with a simple sauce and great texture from slightly crisp, sautéed red cabbage and "meaty" mushrooms. They're so craveable and ready in minutes. You can increase or decrease the spicy heat easily with chili garlic sauce (which also adds great flavor). This sauce would work well with rice noodles or pure soba noodles as well. The ramen noodles are fun to mix things up. Something about their shape and texture is so perfect in this dish.

Servings: 2

6 oz (170 g) dry ramen noodles (one or two ramen "cakes" depending on brand)

1 tsp avocado oil

4 oz (113 g) cremini or portobello mushrooms

¾ cup (53 g) red cabbage, thinly sliced

¼ tsp kosher salt

¼ tsp black pepper

½ tsp garlic powder

2 tsp (10 ml) reduced-sodium soy sauce

½ tsp agave nectar

½ tsp mirin

½ tsp ginger paste

1 tbsp (15 ml) toasted sesame oil

1 tsp chili garlic sauce, plus more for serving

2 tbsp (30 ml) scallions, sliced

To make the noodles, fill a large pot with 2 inches (5 cm) of water, enough to fully submerge the noodles, cover, and bring to a boil. Once boiling, add the noodles, stir, and cover again to bring to a boil. Uncover and continue to boil the noodles, according to the package directions, then drain and rinse them.

Meanwhile, preheat a pan on medium heat and add the avocado oil. Slice the mushrooms and add them to the pan, stir, and cook for 3 to 4 minutes. Add the red cabbage, salt, pepper, and garlic powder to the pan. Cook for 3 minutes, stirring occasionally, as the red cabbage wilts.

While the vegetables cook, to a large mixing bowl, add the soy sauce, agave nectar, mirin, ginger paste, toasted sesame oil, and chili garlic sauce, and whisk together. Add the cooked, drained noodles and toss. Serve the noodles with the vegetables. Top with scallions and more chili garlic sauce, if desired.

Strawberry & Peach Arugula Salad with "Ricotta"

When sweet meets savory, all the good things in life just seem to come together. This Strawberry & Peach Arugula Salad with "Ricotta" has the best of both worlds: juicy and sweet strawberries and peaches, along with savory ricotta and tangy balsamic vinaigrette. The crisp croutons are the topping on the cake, or salad in this case, and they are so perfect to soak up the yummy dressing and for dipping into the creamy ricotta. The salad is so delicious as is, but if you want to kick it up a further notch, add diced avocado, minced red onion or shallot, and toasted sliced almonds or pistachios. You can use store-bought dressing (tip: look for natural ingredients on the label) or whisk up a simple homemade version. It may take you a few more minutes but will be great to have on hand, as the recipe makes a bit extra than you may need for this salad.

Servings: 3 to 4

Salad
3 gently packed cups (8–10 oz) baguette, Italian bread, or sourdough cut into ½-inch (1.3-cm) cubes

1 tsp olive oil, divided

¼ tsp kosher salt

¼ tsp black pepper

¼ tsp garlic powder

1 tsp nutritional yeast

5 oz (142 g) arugula or rocket

½–⅔ cup (120–160 ml) balsamic vinaigrette, store-bought or homemade, divided (see Note)

8 oz (226 g) strawberries, sliced

1½ peaches, thinly sliced

Lemon–Artichoke "Ricotta"
7 oz (198 g) extra-firm tofu

½ tsp kosher salt

¾ tsp garlic powder

Juice of ¾ lemon

1 tsp nutritional yeast

¼ cup (42 g) marinated artichoke hearts, drained

To make the croutons, preheat a large pan on medium heat. Add the bread cubes to the pan with ½ teaspoon of the oil. Season the croutons with the salt, pepper, and garlic powder, and let them cook for 2 to 3 minutes. Then give them a toss, drizzle with the remaining ½ teaspoon of oil, and cook for 2 to 3 minutes, until they're crisp yet soft on the inside. Sprinkle in the nutritional yeast, toss, and let them cool.

While the croutons are cooking, prepare the lemon–artichoke ricotta. Drain the tofu and give it a gentle squeeze with your hands to remove some water. To a food processor, add the tofu, salt, garlic powder, lemon juice, nutritional yeast, and artichoke hearts, and blend them until smooth.

To a large mixing bowl or serving platter, add the arugula and around half of the balsamic vinaigrette and gently toss.

To serve, top the arugula with the strawberries, peaches, dollops of lemon-artichoke ricotta, and crisp croutons, and drizzle with more balsamic vinaigrette as you wish.

Note: You can make a simple and delicious balsamic vinaigrette at home! Simply whisk together the following ingredients in a bowl: ¼ cup (60 ml) of olive oil, ¼ cup (60 ml) of balsamic vinegar, 2 teaspoons (10 ml) of Dijon mustard, 2 teaspoons (10 ml) of agave nectar, ½ teaspoon of garlic powder, 1 teaspoon of kosher salt, and ½ teaspoon of black pepper. This makes a bit more than you'll need for this recipe.

BBQ Jackfruit & Chickpea Flatbread with Creamy Slaw

I have been loving this flatbread ever since making it for the cookbook. It's so flavorful and easy to prepare, with all the right textures. You can use your favorite store-bought BBQ sauce, or I have a super-simple homemade version in the Note below. The combination of the tangy BBQ sauce with the cool slaw along with the crisp flatbread is just so good. Since jackfruit is relatively low in protein on its own, the chickpeas add not only great texture in combination with the jackfruit but also some additional protein.

Servings: 2 to 4

BBQ Jackfruit & Chickpea Flatbread

2 flatbreads or naan

1 (15-oz [425-g]) can young jackfruit

2 tbsp (30 ml) avocado oil

1 cup (164 g) canned chickpeas

⅔ cup (160 ml) BBQ sauce, store-bought or homemade (see Note)

Lime wedges, for serving

Fresh cilantro, for serving

Creamy Slaw

2 packed cups (140 g) coleslaw mix

2 tbsp (30 ml) vegan mayo

2 tbsp (30 ml) plain, unsweetened almond-based yogurt

1 tsp apple cider vinegar

Juice of ½ lemon

½ tsp kosher salt

½ tsp black pepper

½ tsp garlic powder

Preheat the oven to 425°F (220°C). Without waiting for the oven to preheat, place the 2 flatbreads onto a baking tray and place the tray into the oven until the bottom of the bread begins to get crisp, 5 to 8 minutes, depending on the size and thickness of your flatbread, then remove them from the oven. The top of the flatbreads may still be soft.

Meanwhile, preheat a large skillet on medium-high heat. Drain and rinse the jackfruit, discarding the small, oval-shaped cores. Gently shred the jackfruit pieces with your fingers and add them to the pan with the avocado oil. Stir and cook the jackfruit for 5 to 6 minutes, stirring periodically. You want some browning of the jackfruit. Then stir in the chickpeas and BBQ sauce.

While the jackfruit is cooking, make the creamy slaw. To a medium-sized mixing bowl, add the coleslaw mix, mayo, yogurt, vinegar, lemon juice, salt, pepper, and garlic powder, and stir to combine.

Set the oven broiler to high and top the flatbreads with the jackfruit–chickpea mixture, leaving some room around the edges as a crust. Place the tray under the broiler for 1 to 3 minutes, until your desired crispness on the crust. Serve with lime wedges and top the flatbreads with dollops of slaw and cilantro.

Note: While the jackfruit is cooking, you can make a really simple homemade BBQ sauce. Simply add the following ingredients to a small saucepan over medium-high heat, starting with the ketchup, agave nectar, and water, and simmer for 3 to 4 minutes: ½ cup (120 ml) of ketchup, 2 tablespoons (30 ml) of agave nectar, 3 tablespoons (45 ml) of water, ¾ teaspoon of cumin, 1 teaspoon of smoked paprika, ½ teaspoon of onion powder, ¾ teaspoon of fine garlic powder, 1 teaspoon of vegan Worcestershire sauce, ¾ teaspoon of kosher salt, and ½ teaspoon of black pepper.

Sesame Soba Noodles with Citrus Ginger Sauce

Comforting and refreshing soba noodles like these have a special place in my heart. They feel light and satisfying at the same time, and they're so packed with amazing flavors. The Asian-inspired sauce, the quick-pickled cucumbers, the hearty tofu—not to mention the accompaniments of roasted peanuts, scallions, sesame seeds, and kimchi—it's a recipe for deliciousness. Try to get pure buckwheat noodles, which have the most flavor. The pickling of the cucumbers is totally optional but adds some great flavor and is highly recommended.

Servings: 2 to 3

Soba Noodles and Pickled Cucumber

8 oz (226 g) pure soba noodles

10 oz (283 g) super-firm tofu

2 tbsp (30 ml) toasted sesame oil

½ medium seedless cucumber

3 tbsp (45 ml) rice vinegar, for pickling

½ tsp kosher salt, for pickling

1 tsp organic cane sugar, for pickling

2 tsp (10 ml) tamari

½ tsp garlic powder

⅓ cup (49 g) chopped roasted peanuts

2 tbsp (6 g) scallions, thinly sliced

1 tbsp (9 g) black sesame seeds

½ cup (112 g) kimchi, for serving (optional)

Lime wedges, for serving

Sauce

2 tbsp (30 ml) agave nectar

2 tbsp (30 ml) tamari

1½ tbsp (23 ml) lime juice (¾–1 lime)

½ tbsp (8 ml) sambal oelek

1 tbsp (16 g) ginger paste

1 tsp hoisin sauce

To make the soba noodles, fill a large pot with around 2 inches (5 cm) of water, enough to fully submerge the noodles, cover, and bring to a boil. Once the water is boiling, add the noodles, stir, and cover to bring to a boil. Then uncover the pot and continue to boil, according to the package directions. Drain and rinse the noodles.

Meanwhile, preheat a large pan over medium to medium-high heat. Drain the tofu and cut the tofu across its depth to create four thin slabs. Make a crosswise cut across the slabs, then cut those diagonally to create triangles. Add them to the pan along with the toasted sesame oil. Toss the tofu and let it cook for 8 to 10 minutes, flipping halfway and reducing the heat to medium if there's too much browning.

While the tofu is cooking, dice the cucumber and add it to a small bowl along with the vinegar, salt, and sugar. Toss the cucumbers and leave them to marinate while you prepare the rest of the recipe.

During the last couple minutes of the tofu cooking, add in the tamari and garlic powder, and toss. Then transfer the tofu to a plate to cool.

To make the sauce, in a large mixing bowl, add the agave nectar, tamari, lime juice, sambal oelek, ginger paste, and hoisin sauce, and whisk them together. Drain the cucumbers, add them to the bowl, and add the cooked noodles and tofu. Toss everything together. Serve the noodles topped with peanuts, scallions, and sesame seeds. Divide the kimchi between the plates, if using, and serve with a lime wedge on the side.

Chickpea Tempeh Salad Open-Faced Sandwich

This is a great light dinner or lunch meal that always hits the spot. It's hard to imagine that a chickpea and tempeh "salad" can be completely craveable and irresistible, but I kid you not, it is. There's something so yummy about the creamy dressing filled with fresh dill, subtly sweet apricots, and crisp celery—along with amazing flavor additions like Dijon mustard and capers. Add a dash of ground cayenne pepper for a hint of spicy heat, if you like. You can also substitute the apricots for ¼ cup (40 g) of dried cranberries, if you have those handy instead. Feel free to enjoy this like a traditional sandwich topped with lettuce and tomato, or serve the chickpea tempeh salad atop a green salad and your favorite dressing.

Servings: 2 to 3

4 oz (113 g) tempeh

⅓ cup (80 ml) water

1 tsp olive oil

1 cup (164 g) canned chickpeas

1 tbsp (3 g) fresh dill

6 dried apricots

1 medium celery rib

1 tbsp (15 ml) vegan mayo

1 tbsp (15 ml) plain, unsweetened almond-based yogurt

Juice of ½ large lemon

1 tbsp (15 ml) Dijon mustard

½ tsp kosher salt

¾ tsp black pepper

¾ tsp garlic powder

2 tsp (18 g) capers (see Note)

4–6 slices fresh-baked whole wheat bread or sourdough

To prepare the tempeh, place a pan on medium heat. Crumble in the tempeh, leaving some pieces a bit chunkier than others for variation. Add the water and olive oil, cover, and bring to a boil. Then reduce the heat and simmer for 4 to 5 minutes, until the liquid is absorbed. Remove the lid, stir the tempeh, and cook it for 1 to 2 minutes for some browning.

While the tempeh is cooking, drain and rinse the chickpeas, and transfer them to a dinner plate. Roughly mash the chickpeas with a fork, leaving some whole to give some texture. Add them to a large mixing bowl. Chop the fresh dill, thinly slice the apricots, chop the celery, and add them to the bowl.

Add the vegan mayo, yogurt, lemon juice, mustard, salt, pepper, garlic powder, and capers to the chickpeas, along with the cooked tempeh. Give everything a good stir to combine.

Toast the bread, if desired, either in the toaster or under the broiler set to high for 1 to 2 minutes per side. Top the bread with the chickpea–tempeh mixture to serve.

Note: If you don't care for capers, you can substitute with 1 teaspoon of vinegar for extra zing (apple cider vinegar, white wine vinegar, or red wine vinegar), or simply omit.

Warm Kale & Harissa Lentil Salad

A warm lentil salad with greens and an awesome dressing is probably something I could eat every day. The lentils keep me full, and it's a great feeling to know that I'm getting in some greens! Perfectly savory and filled with nutritious ingredients, this salad is likely to be one of your favorites. The harissa paste adds a spicy, almost citrusy burst of flavor in the lentils. I find that harissa paste/sauce can vary in spice level depending on the kind you buy, so start with the small amount and add another teaspoon or two (5 to 10 g) once you taste it with the lentils. This recipe uses fresh mint, but if you're not a fan of mint in savory recipes, feel free to substitute fresh dill or basil.

Servings: 2 to 3

Salad
3 cups (720 ml) vegetable broth
1 cup (192 g) dried sprouted lentils (see Notes)
1–2 tsp (5–10 g) harissa paste, to taste
2 tsp (10 ml) olive oil, divided
1 medium bunch kale
¼ tsp kosher salt
¼ tsp black pepper
1 cup (149 g) cherry or grape tomatoes
1 packed tbsp (6 g) fresh mint
⅓ cup (41 g) roasted pistachios
⅓ cup (50 g) crumbled vegan feta

Tahini Sauce
3 tbsp (45 ml) runny tahini (see Notes)
2 tbsp (30 ml) water
¼–½ tsp kosher salt, to taste
½ tsp garlic powder
Juice of 1 lemon
2 tsp (10 ml) maple syrup

To make the lentils, fill a medium saucepan with the vegetable broth, cover, and bring to a boil. Add the sprouted lentils and cook according to the package directions. Drain away any remaining liquid, and stir the harissa paste and 1 teaspoon of the olive oil into the lentils.

Meanwhile, wash and pat dry the kale, then cut out the tough stems. Cut the kale into small pieces and add it to a large pan placed on medium heat, along with the remaining 1 teaspoon of oil, salt, and pepper. Cook the kale for 3 to 4 minutes, stirring occasionally, until it starts to wilt and turn bright green. Transfer the kale to a serving bowl or tray to cool.

Halve the tomatoes, thinly slice the fresh mint, and coarsely chop the roasted pistachios. Top the kale with the harissa lentils, tomatoes, mint, pistachios, and vegan feta.

For the tahini sauce, to a small bowl, add the tahini, water, salt, garlic powder, lemon juice, and maple syrup, and stir together until they're fully incorporated. Drizzle the salad with the tahini sauce.

Notes: If you can't find sprouted lentils, canned lentils can be used. Alternatively, you can cook regular dried lentil varieties, such as green or black lentils, to al dente, but it will extend the cooking time past 15 minutes. For the recipe, you're looking for 2⅓ cups (462 g) of cooked lentils.

The recipe calls for "runny tahini." Tahini typically comes as either a thick paste or what I'm referring to as the "runny" kind, where the oil separates at the top and when you stir, it's pourable.

Buffalo Chickpea Pitas with Creamy Slaw

These Buffalo Chickpea Pitas are a super-quick meal that's become a go-to! It has great bold flavor, and it's so simple to prepare. These pitas bring the heat in all the best ways. But if super spicy isn't your thing, no worries! You can easily reduce the amount of hot sauce in here; plus, the creamy slaw has a fantastic cool, creamy, and crisp vibe.

Servings: 2

½ small yellow onion

2 tsp (10 ml) avocado oil

2 packed cups (140 g) coleslaw mix

2 tbsp (30 ml) vegan mayo

2 tbsp (30 ml) plain, unsweetened almond-based yogurt

1 tsp apple cider vinegar

Juice of ½ lemon

¾ tsp kosher salt, divided

¾ tsp black pepper, divided

¾ tsp garlic powder, divided

1 (15-oz [425-g]) can chickpeas

¼ tsp paprika

1 packed tbsp (1 g) fresh cilantro

2 tbsp (30 ml) hot sauce, plus more for serving

2 whole wheat pitas (round loaves)

Lime wedges, for serving

To make the pita filling, preheat a pan on medium heat. Finely chop the onion and add it to the pan with the oil. Stir the onion and cook for 4 to 5 minutes.

While the onion cooks, prepare the slaw. To a medium bowl, add the coleslaw mix, vegan mayo, yogurt, apple cider vinegar, and lemon juice, along with ½ teaspoon each of salt, pepper, and garlic powder. Mix the ingredients together until fully combined.

Drain and rinse the chickpeas and add them to the pan with the onion along with the paprika and remaining ¼ teaspoon each of salt, pepper, and garlic powder. Stir the chickpeas and cook them for 2 minutes, until they're heated through, and then remove the pan from the heat. Finely chop the cilantro. Add the cilantro and hot sauce to the pan and stir.

Cut the pitas in half and toast them, then fill them with the chickpeas and coleslaw. Serve it with extra hot sauce and lime wedges to squeeze into the pitas.

Spinach & Mozzarella Stuffed Tortillas

These stuffed tortillas are full of flavor-packed ingredients. And if you're an olive lover, well, this one is dedicated to you. The filling for these tortillas includes fresh herbs, olives, and vegan mozzarella. The dill and parsley give these tortillas a nice freshness, or you can use fresh basil, which would be delicious in here. If you're in the mood to jazz it up or have an accompaniment to the stuffed tortillas, I'm including a recipe for a quick yet super-flavorful tomato, cucumber, and olive salad. The contrasting crisp cucumber and savory olives make a yummy pair for these stuffed tortillas.

Servings: 2

1 large clove garlic

½ tsp olive oil, plus more for tortillas

1½ packed cups (43 g) baby spinach

Pinch of kosher salt and black pepper

1 packed tbsp (3 g) fresh dill

1 packed tbsp (4 g) fresh parsley

⅓ cup (56 g) marinated artichokes, drained

2 green olives, pitted

4 (10-inch [25-cm]) round flour tortillas, regular or whole wheat, divided

⅔ packed cup (74 g) vegan mozzarella

Pinch of red chili flakes

Tomato, Cucumber, & Olive Salad (optional)

1 cup (149 g) cherry or grape tomatoes

¼ medium seedless cucumber

6 green olives, pitted

2 tsp (10 ml) olive oil

1 tsp balsamic vinegar

¼ tsp garlic powder

¼ tsp kosher salt

¼ tsp black pepper

To make the garlicky spinach, preheat a large skillet on medium heat. Mince the garlic and add it to the pan with the oil, baby spinach, and a pinch of salt and pepper. Stir and cook for around 2 minutes until it is fully wilted, then transfer it to a plate. While the spinach is cooking, finely chop the dill and parsley. Coarsely chop the marinated artichokes and olives.

You'll need two skillets to make both servings at the same time. Alternatively, you can use small tortillas and a very large pan, which may fit three small tortillas at once depending on the size of your pan. On medium heat, add a touch of oil to the skillets, or use nonstick skillets. Place half the tortillas in the skillets and spread most of the mozzarella across the tortillas, reserving some cheese. Top the tortillas with the artichokes, olives, and most of the fresh dill and parsley. You can reserve some for the tomato, cucumber, and olive salad.

Top the tortillas with the remaining cheese and a pinch of red chili flakes, then place a second tortilla on top. When the bottom tortilla is becoming golden brown in places, 2 to 3 minutes, gently flip and cook the other side for 1 to 2 minutes, until it is lightly golden brown.

While the tortillas are cooking, you can prepare the tomato, cucumber, and olive salad if you've chosen to make it. Dice the tomatoes and cucumber. Add them to a large bowl with the olives, olive oil, balsamic vinegar, garlic powder, salt, pepper, and remaining fresh herbs. Toss and taste for seasoning.

Slice the finished stuffed tortillas in half or quarters, and serve them with the salad on the side, if using.

Smoky Mushroom, Pinto, & Corn Tacos

These smoky, rich, and hearty tacos are a yummy twist on traditional tacos with a quick and easy sauce that is combined with mushrooms, corn, and pinto beans. Tip: You can use presliced mushrooms if you like, to make this recipe even faster. Crunchy taco shells are a perfect way to serve these tacos, as the crisp shells complement the creamy veggie and bean filling just perfectly. They're topped off with avocado and cilantro, and I like to serve these with lots of lime wedges and fresh tomato. If you don't have pinto beans, a great substitute would be black beans.

Servings: 3 to 4

8 oz (226 g) cremini or baby portobello mushrooms

1 tbsp (15 ml) avocado oil

¼ red onion

⅓ cup (45 g) frozen corn

1 (15-oz [425-g]) can pinto beans, drained and rinsed

⅔ cup (160 ml) BBQ sauce, store-bought or homemade (see Note)

1 lime

6–8 crunchy taco shells

1 avocado, sliced

2 tbsp (2 g) cilantro

1 cup (180 g) chopped tomatoes

Preheat a large pan over medium-high heat. Slice the mushrooms and add them to the pan with the oil. Let them cook for 1 to 2 minutes while slicing the red onion. Add the onion to the pan, stir, and cook for 5 to 6 minutes. A little browning is good. Add the corn and pinto beans, stir, and cook for 2 to 3 minutes.

Carefully stir the BBQ sauce into the vegetable and bean mixture. Cut the lime into wedges, then divide the taco filling mixture between the taco shells. Serve them with the lime wedges, sliced avocado, fresh cilantro, and tomatoes as toppings for the tacos.

Note: While the vegetables are cooking, you can make a really simple homemade BBQ sauce. Simply add the following ingredients to a small saucepan over medium-high heat, starting with the ketchup, agave nectar, and water, and simmer it for 3 to 4 minutes: ½ cup (120 ml) of ketchup, 2 tablespoons (30 ml) of agave nectar, 3 tablespoons (45 ml) of water, ¾ teaspoon of cumin, 1 teaspoon of smoked paprika, ½ teaspoon of onion powder, ¾ teaspoon of garlic powder, 1 teaspoon of vegan Worcestershire sauce, ¾ teaspoon of kosher salt, and ½ teaspoon of black pepper.

Hummus Toast with Vegetables & Basil

This scrumptious toast feels fancy and is ready in a snap—the best of both worlds! It's full of flavor from sautéed mushrooms and zucchini, along with a lemony, olive oil hummus that is super fast to make in the food processor. It is also hearty enough to be a delicious dinner option, thanks to the satisfying hummus. The toasts are topped with roasted pistachios, fresh basil, and some extra lemon juice for a savory meal. The hummus is a shortcut version and uses olive oil rather than more traditional preparations that use tahini. Feel free to substitute half of the olive oil for tahini. I hope this recipe gives you inspiration to try different combinations of fresh herbs and nuts, and even for the vegetables. For example, the toasts would also be delicious with sautéed leeks, bells peppers, or onions. Feel free to use your choice of bread. This version uses bakery bread that I sliced fairly thick, and you can either toast the slices in the toaster or under the broiler.

Serves: 3

¼ cup + 1 tbsp (75 ml) olive oil, divided

4 medium cremini or baby portobello mushrooms

1 medium zucchini

1 tsp kosher salt, divided

¾ tsp black pepper, divided

1 tsp garlic powder, divided

1 (15-oz [425-g]) can chickpeas

1½ lemons, divided

6 thick slices fresh country bread

Fresh basil

Chopped pistachios, for serving

To make the vegetables, preheat a large pan on medium heat and add 1 tablespoon (15 ml) of the olive oil. Slice the mushrooms, then add them to the pan and toss. Let them cook for 2 minutes while preparing the zucchini. Cut the zucchini in a small dice and add it to the pan, along with ¼ teaspoon of salt, ½ teaspoon of black pepper, and ½ teaspoon of garlic powder. Stir everything together and let it cook for 5 to 6 minutes, stirring halfway. Some browning is good to add flavor.

While the vegetables are cooking, prepare the hummus. Drain and rinse the chickpeas and add them to a food processor. Add in the remaining ¼ cup (60 ml) of olive oil, juice of 1 lemon, and the remaining ¾ teaspoon of salt, ¼ teaspoon of pepper, and ½ teaspoon of garlic powder. Blend the hummus until smooth, scraping down the sides as needed.

Toast the slices of bread in the toaster or under the broiler set on high, broiling for 1 to 2 minutes per side on a baking tray. Thinly slice the basil leaves.

To serve, spread the hummus on the bread slices and top with the vegetable mixture, basil, and pistachios. Squeeze the juice of the remaining ½ lemon over top.

Spicy & Cheesy Chickpea & Mushroom Flatbread

This Spicy & Cheesy Chickpea & Mushroom Flatbread is a delicious dish to try for your next pizza night at home. It's topped with nourishing ingredients like chickpeas and mushrooms (of course), plus corn, red onion, and seasonings. At the end, we add hot sauce for some spicy heat, and it makes a perfect flavor complement to the other toppings. This recipe is one of my husband's favorites from the cookbook! You can use your preference of flatbread or naan and simply cook it to your desired crispness. The initial crisping of the flatbread step is optional. Alternatively, you can simply broil the flatbread with the toppings in the later step. The flatbread will still be soft, letting you fold it over as you eat it. The sliced tomato in this recipe is optional too. Great with tomato, great without!

Servings: 3 to 4

2 flatbreads or naan

4 medium–large cremini or baby portobello mushrooms

1 tbsp (15 ml) avocado oil

¼ red onion

⅓ cup (45 g) frozen corn

1 cup (164 g) canned chickpeas, drained and rinsed

½ tsp chili powder

½ tsp kosher salt

½ tsp garlic powder

½ tsp ground cumin

½ medium tomato (optional)

⅓ cup (37 g) shredded vegan mozzarella

⅓ cup (37 g) shredded vegan cheddar

1 tbsp (1 g) cilantro (see Note)

2–3 tbsp (30–45 ml) hot sauce, to taste

To crisp the flatbread, set the oven to 425°F (220°C) and place the flatbreads on a baking tray. Place the tray into the oven while preparing the toppings, without waiting for the oven to preheat. When the flatbreads start to get crisp on the bottom, 5 to 8 minutes, remove the tray from the oven. The top of the flatbreads may still be soft.

Meanwhile, preheat a large pan on medium-high heat. Slice the mushrooms and add them to the pan with the avocado oil. Stir and let them cook for 1 to 2 minutes while you slice the red onion. Add these to the pan, stir, and cook for 2 minutes. Next, add the corn, chickpeas, chili powder, salt, garlic powder, and cumin. Stir and cook for 2 to 3 minutes.

Set the oven broiler to high. Thinly slice the tomato, if using, and lay it on the crispy-bottomed flatbreads, leaving room for an outer crust, then spread the vegetable mixture across the flatbreads. Top them evenly with vegan mozzarella and cheddar, then place the tray under the broiler for 1 to 3 minutes. The cheese will melt slightly and the flatbread crusts will start to turn golden brown.

While the flatbreads are in the oven, finely chop the cilantro. Remove the flatbreads from the oven and top them with hot sauce and cilantro.

Note: If you don't like cilantro, feel free to use fresh parsley instead, or omit it.

Pesto & White Bean Hummus Flatbread

Flatbreads are a staple in our house when we're looking for a quick yet really satisfying lunch or dinner. The topping possibilities are endless too! For this one, we top the flatbread with two of my favorites: hummus and pesto! Can it get any better? There're also roasted red peppers, dill, olives, and za'atar seasoning to add tons of Mediterranean-inspired flavors. This flatbread is a flavor explosion, and I hope you'll love it as much as I do!

Servings: 3 to 4

2 flatbreads or naan

1 (15-oz [425-g]) can cannellini beans

2 tbsp (30 ml) olive oil

1 large clove garlic

¼–½ tsp kosher salt

½ tsp black pepper

1 lemon, divided

2 tbsp (23 g) pitted Kalamata olives

½ cup (160 g) roasted red peppers, drained well

½ cup (120 ml) vegan pesto, store-bought or homemade (see Note)

1 tsp za'atar seasoning, for serving (optional)

Fresh dill finely chopped, for serving (optional)

Preheat the oven to 425°F (220°C). Without waiting for the oven to preheat, place the flatbreads onto a baking tray and into the oven until the bottom becomes crisp, 5 to 8 minutes depending on the size and thickness of your flatbread, then remove them from the oven. The top of the flatbreads may still be soft. If you'd like a crisper flatbread, bake for another 2 to 4 minutes.

Meanwhile, prepare the white bean hummus. Drain and rinse the cannellini beans. Add the beans, olive oil, garlic, salt, pepper, and juice of half the lemon to a food processor. Cut the remaining half of the lemon into wedges for serving. Blend the hummus until smooth, scraping down the sides as needed. Transfer the hummus to a bowl.

Coarsely chop the olives and roasted red peppers. Assemble the flatbreads by spreading around ¼ cup (60 ml) of the hummus on each flatbread, leaving some crust open around the edge. Top the hummus with the olives and roasted peppers, then top with several tablespoons (30 ml) of the pesto on each flatbread. Sprinkle the za'atar seasoning and fresh dill on top, if using.

Note: You can make a homemade mixed-herb pistachio pesto that will be delicious for this flatbread. Blend it up in the food processor after making the hummus, and it will take just a few extra minutes to prepare. Simply blend the following ingredients: 1½ packed tablespoons (4 g) of fresh basil, ¾ medium bunch of fresh dill, 1½ packed tablespoons (2 g) of fresh parsley, ¼ cup (60 ml) of olive oil, 1 large clove of garlic, 2 tablespoons (30 ml) of lemon juice (about 1 lemon), ¼ to ½ teaspoon of kosher salt, ½ teaspoon of pepper, ¼ cup (31 g) of shelled roasted pistachios, and ½ cup (57 g) of vegan Parmesan shreds (or ⅓ cup [33 g] of grated vegan Parmesan).

Mushroom & Tempeh Lettuce Cups

These Mushroom & Tempeh Lettuce Cups are fun and flavorful, loaded with fresh herbs, a savory sauce, and crunchy roasted peanuts. Serve them with lots of lime wedges, along with extra chili garlic sauce to turn up the heat, if you like things spicy. The butter lettuce leaves make a perfect wrap for these cups. The filling is primarily made of diced mushrooms and tempeh, which provide protein and nutrients. Buy presliced mushrooms if you can, to save time chopping. Alternatively, you can add the mushrooms to a food processor and pulse several times until they're chopped, and it's okay if the pieces are different sizes. Serving tip: Either assemble and enjoy these lettuce cups right away, or if you're not quite ready to dig in, let the filling mixture cool a bit before filling the cups to avoid the lettuce wilting.

Servings: 3 to 4

Lettuce Cups

1½ tbsp (23 ml) toasted sesame oil

10–12 butter lettuce leaves

8 oz (226 g) package tempeh

8 oz (226 g) cremini or baby portobello mushrooms

¾ cup (240 g) roasted red peppers, drained well

1 packed tbsp (1 g) fresh cilantro

1 packed tbsp (6 g) fresh mint (optional)

2 stalks scallions (optional)

⅓ cup (49 g) chopped roasted peanuts

1 lime, cut into wedges, for serving

Sauce

¼ cup (60 ml) reduced-sodium soy sauce

1 tbsp (15 ml) mirin

1½ tbsp (23 ml) agave nectar

2 tsp (10 g) ginger paste

½ tsp garlic powder

1 tsp cornstarch

1 tbsp (15 ml) lime juice (½–¾ lime)

1–1½ tbsp (15–23 ml) chili garlic sauce, to taste

Preheat a large skillet on medium-high heat and add the oil. Lay out the butter lettuce leaves on a couple of plates, ready to fill later. Crumble the tempeh block into the pan with your hands, being careful of oil splatter. Stir the tempeh, reduce the heat to medium, and let it cook for 1 to 2 minutes.

Meanwhile, coarsely chop the mushrooms and add them to the pan. Stir everything and cook for 7 to 8 minutes, partially covered, stirring periodically. Some browning is fine.

While the tempeh and mushrooms are cooking, slice the roasted red peppers, cilantro, mint, if using, and the scallions, if using.

To make the sauce, to a small bowl, add the soy sauce, mirin, agave, ginger paste, garlic powder, cornstarch, lime juice, and chili garlic sauce, and whisk them together.

Add the sauce and roasted red peppers to the pan. As you stir everything together, the sauce will quickly thicken, likely within 1 minute. To serve, divide the mixture between the lettuce leaves. Top with the cilantro, mint, scallions, and peanuts, and serve the lettuce cups with lime wedges.

Warm Lentil & Carrot Salad with Herbs & Balsamic Vinaigrette

Sometimes lentils get a bad reputation for being bland or just plain boring. But in this Warm Lentil & Carrot Salad with Herbs and Balsamic Vinaigrette, the lentils are cooked to al dente, seasoned to perfection, and served in a savory balsamic vinaigrette. The carrots give some great sweetness to the lentils, and the red onion adds a mild kick. It's great with either baby spinach, spring mix/leafy green mix, or arugula/rocket. This salad is one that you'll want to make again and again, and it's so tasty yet so quick and nourishing. If you know you'll have leftovers or would like to make this in advance, keep the baby spinach separate until serving. The warm lentils wilt the spinach, which works well for serving immediately, but for leftovers you may prefer them crisper.

Servings: 3 to 4

Salad
1 cup (192 g) dried sprouted lentils (see Note)

3 cups (720 ml) vegetable broth

1 cup (110 g) thinly sliced carrots

1½ tbsp (23 ml) olive oil

½ medium–large red onion

1 tsp kosher salt

1 tsp black pepper

1 tsp garlic powder

1 cup (149 g) cherry or grape tomatoes

3 packed cups (85 g) baby spinach

Vinaigrette
2 tbsp (30 ml) olive oil

2 tbsp (30 ml) balsamic vinegar

1 tbsp (15 ml) agave nectar

1 tbsp (15 ml) Dijon mustard

To make the lentils, add the lentils and the vegetable broth to a medium saucepan and bring it to a boil, covered. Cook until al dente, then drain any remaining broth away and give them a quick rinse in cold water to cool them down somewhat.

Meanwhile, preheat a pan on medium heat and add the carrots and olive oil. Stir and let these cook for 2 to 3 minutes, partially covered. Thinly slice the red onion, and add it to the pan with the salt, pepper, and garlic powder. Stir and let the vegetables cook for 5 to 6 minutes, partially covered, stirring periodically. Some browning is fine, and the vegetables can have some bite to them for texture.

While the vegetables cook, make the vinaigrette. In a small bowl, whisk together the olive oil, balsamic vinegar, agave nectar, and mustard.

Halve the cherry tomatoes. Serve the lentils on top of the baby spinach, along with the tomatoes, carrots, and onion. Add the vinaigrette and toss. The baby spinach will wilt a bit under the warm lentils.

Note: If you can't find sprouted lentils, canned lentils can be used. Alternatively, you can cook regular dried lentil varieties like green or black lentils, cooked to al dente, but it will extend the cooking time past 15 minutes. For the recipe, you're looking for 2⅓ cups (462 g) of cooked lentils.

Fajita-Spiced Portobello Burgers with Avocado

These yummy portobello burgers are a great plant-based alternative to beef burgers, with chewy mushroom texture and bold seasoning. The spice mix adds great flavor and makes a perfect pair for the refreshing tomato salad that tops the burgers, along with creamy avocado. I love this burger option for a light meal that celebrates how delicious mushrooms can be in their simplicity. Share it with the mushroom lovers in your life, and bonus points if you do it in an outdoor summer cookout situation.

Servings: 2 to 4

Burgers
1½ tbsp (23 ml) avocado oil

3 large portobello mushroom caps

½ tsp garlic powder

½ tsp chili powder

¼ tsp kosher salt

½ tsp black pepper

½ tsp ground cumin

1 avocado

4 burger buns

Tomato Salad
¾ cup (112 g) cherry or grape tomatoes

1½ tbsp (15 g) finely chopped red onion

⅛ tsp kosher salt

⅛ tsp black pepper

½ tsp olive oil

½ tbsp (8 ml) lime juice (¼–½ lime)

1 packed tbsp (1 g) fresh cilantro

To make the mushrooms, preheat a large pan on medium-high heat and add the oil. Slice the mushroom caps into thin strips, approximately ½ inch (1.3 cm) thick. Add these to the pan and cook them for 4 to 6 minutes, stirring occasionally, until they begin to brown.

While the mushrooms are cooking, to a small bowl, add the garlic powder, chili powder, salt, pepper, and cumin, and stir together. Sprinkle the seasonings on the mushrooms, toss them, and cook for an additional 2 to 4 minutes on medium heat. You want the mushrooms to release any water and continue to brown.

Meanwhile, prepare the tomato salad. Slice the tomatoes in halves or quarters, depending on size, and add them to a medium bowl, including their juices. Add the finely chopped red onion, salt, pepper, olive oil, and lime juice. Finely chop the fresh cilantro and stir it in. Slice the avocado, for serving.

Toast the burger buns, if desired, in the toaster or under a broiler. To broil, place the bun halves on a baking tray and place the tray under the broiler set to high for 1 to 2 minutes, or just until they are golden brown, flip, and broil another minute. Divide the mushrooms among the burger buns and top the mushrooms with the tomato salad and avocado.

Warming Soups & Cozy Curries

Ahhh, soups and curries. Welcome to my happy place! It doesn't matter what time of year—if the soup craving hits, it hits! Soups and curries are one of those things that are often thought to be cooked over time, and in some cases, the longer the better. For this book, I've done my best to bring you a collection of amazing soups and stews that come together in a very short amount of time yet still bring all the flavor, vibrance, and in some cases, decadence. (Cue the Creamy Mushroom, Chickpea, & Sun-Dried Tomato Soup [page 90] and my Cozy White Bean & Spinach Soup [page 98]).

Or, if you are in the mood for a warm hug in soup form that still feels light and fresh, you can whip up the Udon Ginger Miso Soup with Vegetables (page 89) or the Smoky Pinto Bean, Mushroom, & Tomato Soup (page 97).

There are multiple different cuisines that inspired the recipes in this chapter, including the Thai-inspired Ginger Noodle & Vegetable Red Curry Soup (page 81) and the Indian-inspired Lentil & Mushroom Curry with Spinach & Tomatoes (page 94). So, get ready for a delicious variety of quick and tasty bowls that are hearty enough for dinner, yet easy on your time.

Ginger Noodle & Vegetable Red Curry Soup

This Ginger Noodle & Vegetable Red Curry Soup is so full of flavor, you may find yourself grabbing an extra bowl. It's filled with extra-satisfying ingredients that will not disappoint for a super-fast dinner. Textured vegetable protein (TVP) may be difficult to find in stores, so go for it online. Alternatively, you can substitute beans, such as great northern beans, or double up on the shiitake mushrooms. The soup gets additional flavor from fresh garlic, ginger paste, turmeric, and coconut milk. If you haven't guessed already, this recipe is ultra-warming and will leave you craving more!

Servings: 3 to 4

1 large shallot

½ red bell pepper

1 tbsp (15 ml) avocado oil, divided

1 medium zucchini

3 large cloves garlic

¼ cup (66 g) Thai red curry paste

2 tsp (10 g) ginger paste, plus more to taste

3 cups (720 ml) vegetable broth (see Note)

1 (15-oz [425-g]) can full-fat coconut milk

¼ tsp turmeric

¼ tsp black pepper

½ cup (50 g) dry textured vegetable protein (also known as TVP)

4 oz (113 g) dry ramen noodles

3.5 oz (100 g) shiitake mushrooms

1 tbsp (15 ml) lemon juice (about ½ lemon)

2 tbsp (2 g) fresh cilantro, for serving (optional)

Chili garlic sauce, for serving (optional)

Preheat a large pan or skillet on medium heat. Finely chop the shallot and slice the red bell pepper. Add these to the pan, along with 2 teaspoons (10 ml) of the oil. Stir and let them cook for approximately 2 minutes while you prepare the zucchini and garlic.

Trim the ends off the zucchini. Slice the zucchini lengthwise, then make slices crosswise to make half-moon shapes. Mince the garlic, then add the zucchini and garlic to the pan. Cook for 1 to 2 minutes, then add the red curry paste, ginger paste, vegetable broth, coconut milk, turmeric, pepper, TVP, and dry ramen noodles. Bring it to a boil, covering and raising the heat if needed, then lower the heat and cook at a gentle simmer, uncovered, for approximately 3 minutes, until the ramen noodles are tender.

While the soup is cooking, preheat a small skillet on medium-high heat. Remove the stems of the shiitake mushrooms, then slice the caps. Add the mushrooms to the pan with the remaining 1 teaspoon of oil and cook for 2 to 3 minutes, stirring occasionally.

When you're ready to serve, stir the lemon juice into the soup. If you're a ginger lover, stir in a bit more ginger paste. To serve, divide the soup into bowls and top with the mushrooms, fresh cilantro, if using, and chili garlic sauce, if desired, for spicy heat.

Note: To thin the soup, you can add an additional ½ to 1 cup (120 to 240 ml) of vegetable broth, which would be a total of 4 cups (960 ml) of broth.

Chickpea, Corn, & Spinach Curry

This curry is a tried-and-true favorite in our house! Who doesn't love a cozy, warm, delectable bowl of curry? It has a super-creamy and simple sauce that is surprisingly flavorful for coming together in 15 minutes. This quick preparation is definitely not traditional, but it pays homage to the beautiful Indian flavors that I love. The spices in this curry are a winning combination, with a hint of cinnamon and a mild amount of heat. If you'd like to cut down on the spicy heat, go ahead and halve the chili powder. It will still be delicious!

Servings: 4

1 cup (200 g) jasmine rice

1 small onion

1½ tbsp (23 ml) avocado oil or other neutral oil

3 large cloves garlic

1 cup (149 g) cherry or grape tomatoes

1 cup (136 g) frozen corn

2 tsp (6 g) garlic powder

1 tsp kosher salt

1 tbsp (6 g) curry powder

1 tbsp (6 g) ground cumin

¼ tsp ground ginger

¼ tsp cinnamon (optional)

1 tsp chili powder

1¾ tsp (4 g) ground coriander

¾ cup (180 g) canned crushed tomatoes

1 (15-oz [425-g]) can full-fat coconut milk

1 (15-oz [425-g]) can chickpeas, drained and rinsed

2 cups (60 g) baby spinach

In a medium saucepan, add the jasmine rice and 2 cups (480 ml) of water. Bring to a boil, covered, then immediately reduce the heat to low and cook until the rice is tender and the water has evaporated, around 12 minutes.

Preheat a large pan on medium heat, then finely chop the onion. Add the onion and oil to the pan, stir, and let it cook for 5 minutes, stirring periodically. Meanwhile, mince the garlic and halve the cherry tomatoes. Add the garlic, cherry tomatoes, corn, garlic powder, salt, curry powder, cumin, ground ginger, cinnamon, if using, chili powder, and coriander to the pan. Stir and cook for 1 minute, then add the crushed tomatoes, coconut milk, and chickpeas.

Stir the curry and bring it to a boil, covered, then lower the heat to a simmer, uncovered, for another few minutes. During the last minute, stir in the baby spinach to wilt. Serve with the jasmine rice.

Chunky Tomato & Cannellini Spinach Soup

This one goes out to all the tomato fans who love the sweet yet savory taste in these little gems of nature. I can't think of a much better situation than cozying up with a hot bowl of this Chunky Tomato & Cannellini Spinach Soup in the cooler months, with some vegan Parmesan sprinkled on top. The fresh and dried herbs, onion, and tomato paste help build flavor in a short time, along with the capers to serve with, for a little zing. The cherry tomatoes, white beans, sun-dried tomatoes, and baby spinach make this soup super chunky and rich, while nourishing, too.

Servings: 3 to 4

½ medium onion

1 tsp kosher salt

½ tsp black pepper

2 tbsp (30 ml) olive oil (see Notes)

1½ cups (224 g) cherry or grape tomatoes

⅓ cup (76 g) sun-dried tomatoes packed in oil, drained

2 cups (480 ml) vegetable broth (see Note)

1 (15-oz [425-g]) can cannellini beans, drained and rinsed

3 tbsp (48 g) tomato paste

1 tsp dried oregano

1 tsp garlic powder

1 packed tbsp (4 g) fresh parsley

2 packed cups (60 g) baby spinach

1 tbsp (9 g) capers, or to taste

2 sprigs fresh thyme, for serving (optional)

Grated vegan Parmesan, for serving (optional)

Preheat a large pot or deep pan over medium-high heat. Finely chop the onion and add it to the pan with the salt, pepper, and olive oil. Stir the onion and let it cook it for 2 to 3 minutes while preparing the tomatoes. Halve the cherry tomatoes and add them to the pan. Cover the pan and cook the tomatoes for 3 to 4 minutes.

Meanwhile, finely chop the sun-dried tomatoes. Add them to the pan with the vegetable broth, cannellini beans, tomato paste, dried oregano, and garlic powder. Bring the soup to a boil, covered, then uncover and reduce the heat to a simmer, and cook for 1 to 2 minutes.

Finely chop the fresh parsley. Add the parsley and baby spinach to the pan, stir, and cook for 1 to 2 minutes until the spinach wilts. Serve the soup and top it with the capers, along with the fresh thyme and vegan Parmesan, if using.

Notes: For a decadent touch, drizzle in a bit more olive oil at the end.

To thin the soup, add another ½ cup (120 ml) of vegetable broth.

Hearty Black-Eyed Peas & Kale Soup

This cozy and hearty soup has been on repeat here, and that's saying something—since it's the middle of summer while I'm writing this. It makes a really great meal prep soup that you can reach for during busy evenings. It's also so comforting. The kale will not stay as bright green for leftovers, but it holds its texture and flavor well. This soup is packed with satiating and nourishing ingredients like black-eyed peas, bell peppers, and kale. This combination, plus the warming herbs and spices, makes for a totally crave-worthy soup. I know . . . kale can be crave-worthy? Thankfully, yes! Other delicious examples of this unlikely phenomenon are the Angel Hair with Lemon, Kale, & Tomatoes (page 18) and the Spiced Chickpea & Kale Salad with Vegan Honey Mustard (page 47).

Servings: 3 to 4

½ medium yellow onion

1 tsp kosher salt

1 tbsp (15 ml) neutral oil, such as avocado oil

1 tbsp (14 g) plant-based butter

1 bell pepper

½ tsp ground cumin

2½ tsp (3 g) Italian seasoning blend

1½ tsp (4 g) garlic powder

1½ tsp (3 g) paprika

Pinch of cayenne (optional)

1 cup (240 g) canned crushed tomatoes

1 (15-oz [425-g]) can black-eyed peas, drained and rinsed

2 cups (480 ml) vegetable broth

2 medium kale leaves

1 tsp agave nectar (optional)

1 tbsp (3 g) dried or fresh chives, for serving (optional)

Crusty bread, for serving (optional)

Preheat a large pot over medium heat. Finely chop the onion and add it to the pot, along with the salt, oil, and plant-based butter. Cook the onion for 2 to 3 minutes.

Meanwhile, finely chop the bell pepper. Add the bell pepper, cumin, Italian seasoning, garlic powder, paprika, and cayenne. Stir the vegetables and cook for 2 to 3 minutes, then add the crushed tomatoes, black-eyed peas, and vegetable broth.

Stir the soup, cover, and bring it to a boil while preparing the kale. Chop the kale into small bite-sized pieces, removing any tough stems. Add the kale to the pot, stir, and cook for 2 minutes as the kale wilts. Stir in the agave nectar, if using, then serve topped with chives, if desired. Crusty bread with plant-based butter is a yummy serving option!

Udon Ginger Miso Soup with Vegetables

This warming, cozy, and simple soup will really hit the spot for a light meal in any season. Chewy, satisfying udon noodles along with umami-packed miso and wakame flakes are so perfect with your favorite vegetable broth, tofu, and colorful veggies. This soup makes great leftovers, too, so feel free to double the batch. I find myself looking forward to this soup, and I hope that you will too! Check for the dried wakame in the Asian section of your local grocery store, at Asian markets, or online. If you can't find them, you can use a nori sheet cut into small squares. Start with a smaller amount than the dried wakame flakes, as the nori gives more robust flavor. If you haven't used precooked udon noodles before, they're available in packages. You simply remove them from the package and add them to the broth. Sometimes the noodle packages come with a flavor packet, which you can discard.

Servings: 3

4 cups (960 ml) vegetable broth

1 heaping tbsp (4 g) dried wakame flakes

½ red bell pepper

1¼ cups (170 g) frozen corn

8 oz (226 g) soft tofu

7 oz (198 g) precooked udon noodles

½ tbsp (8 g) ginger paste (see Notes)

¼ cup (66 g) white miso paste (see Notes)

1 tbsp (15 ml) sambal oelek or chili garlic sauce, plus more to taste, for spicy heat (optional)

1 cup (30 g) baby spinach

To a large pot over medium heat, add the vegetable broth to warm it up while preparing the dried wakame flakes. Add the wakame flakes to a small bowl, and add enough warm water to cover the flakes to rehydrate them. After 3 to 5 minutes, squeeze the water out and set them aside.

Meanwhile, finely chop the bell pepper and add it to the broth. Add the frozen corn, cover, and let the broth heat for approximately 2 minutes while preparing the tofu. If the broth begins to boil, lower the heat to keep the broth at a very low simmer. Cut the tofu into thin slabs, then place the slabs on top of each other and cut in strips lengthwise, then crosswise to create small pieces, approximately ½ inch (1.3 cm) thick. Add the udon noodles and ginger paste to the broth. Stir the broth, cover, and bring it to a boil, then simmer for 2 to 3 minutes.

While the broth is simmering, in a medium bowl, add the miso along with 1 cup (240 ml) of the hot broth from the pot. Whisk these together to dissolve the miso, then add it back to the pot, along with the rehydrated wakame flakes, tofu cubes, and sambal oelek, if using. Stir the baby spinach into the soup, and serve the soup with more sambal oelek to taste.

Notes: Store-bought ginger paste can vary since some may include other flavors. Add more ginger paste if you like.

You can add more or less white miso paste to taste. The miso gives an umami, salty flavor.

Creamy Mushroom, Chickpea, & Sun-Dried Tomato Soup

This Creamy Mushroom, Chickpea, & Sun-Dried Tomato Soup has some serious flavor. It's creamy, it's savory, and it's so good. It may look like a lot of ingredients, but the vast majority of them get thrown in all at the same time to the savory one-pot deliciousness. Fragrant sautéed leeks and mushrooms start the base of the soup, with other amazing additions like chickpeas, sun-dried tomatoes, and marinated artichoke hearts. The artichoke hearts may sound like an unlikely ingredient for soup, but I hope you'll find (like I did) that they were meant for this soup, in all their glory. You can alternatively use the non-marinated variety of artichoke hearts, which are usually unseasoned. Therefore, you may want to increase the dried seasonings a bit. For example, add a dash more garlic powder, pepper, and dried oregano for extra flavor.

Servings: 4 to 5

1 tbsp (15 ml) olive oil

1 tbsp (14 g) plant-based butter

8 oz (226 g) presliced baby portobello mushrooms

1 leek

⅓ cup (76 g) sun-dried tomatoes packed in oil, drained

½ cup (98 g) marinated artichoke hearts, drained

1 (15-oz [425-g]) can chickpeas, drained and rinsed

1 cup (240 ml) canned full-fat coconut milk

1½ cups (360 g) vegetable broth (see Note)

3 tbsp (48 g) tomato paste

1 tsp kosher salt

1 tsp black pepper

1 tsp garlic powder

½ tsp dried tarragon

½ tsp Italian seasoning blend

2 tbsp (8 g) finely chopped fresh parsley, for serving (optional)

Red chili flakes, for serving (optional)

Heat a large pot or deep pan on medium-high heat and add the olive oil, butter, and mushrooms. Stir and let the mushrooms cook for 5 minutes while preparing the leek. Some browning is fine, as it adds flavor.

To prepare the leek, cut the bottom stem part off the leek and slice the entire leek lengthwise, then thinly slice the light green part crosswise to create half-moon shapes. You'll need 1 cup (94 g) of sliced leek. Some white/dark green parts are fine. Rinse the sliced leek under running water, then add it to the pan. Stir the vegetables, and let them continue to cook for 2 to 4 minutes.

Meanwhile, finely chop the sun-dried tomatoes and chop the artichoke hearts. Add these and the chickpeas, coconut milk, broth, tomato paste, salt, pepper, garlic powder, tarragon, and Italian seasoning to the pan, and stir together. Once all the ingredients have been added, cook them together for 1 to 2 minutes. Serve the soup with chopped parsley and red chili flakes, if desired.

Note: For a thinner soup, add an additional ½ to 1 cup (120 to 240 ml) more water or vegetable broth.

Creamy Tomato Soup with Pesto Grilled Cheese

This is the ultimate soup and sandwich combination, and you can make it at home in no time at all. Imagine creamy and tangy tomato soup paired with a grilled cheese sandwich that is crisp and filled with all the goodness of herby pesto and vegan cheese. You can use store-bought vegan pesto, but I've also shared a quick recipe for my favorite homemade pesto in the Notes. It is worth taking the extra minute or two to whip up, as it really takes things to the next level. I also use it in the Pesto & White Bean Hummus Flatbread (page 71). Try to use the best quality canned crushed tomatoes you can. It will make the flavors in this creamy tomato soup really shine.

Servings: 2 to 3

½ medium yellow onion

1 tbsp (15 ml) olive oil, plus more for toasting the bread

1 tsp kosher salt

½ tsp black pepper

1 tsp garlic powder

1 (28-oz [784-g]) can crushed tomatoes

½ tbsp (8 ml) agave nectar

2 tbsp (30 ml) coconut cream (see Notes)

4 slices fresh baked whole wheat or sourdough

⅓ cup (37 g) vegan mozzarella shreds

⅔ cup (160 ml) pesto, homemade or store-bought (see Notes)

To make the soup, preheat a pan on medium heat and finely chop the onion. Add it to the pan with the oil, salt, and pepper. Stir and cook the onion for 5 to 6 minutes, stirring periodically, until the onion is softening. Stir in the garlic powder, crushed tomatoes, and agave nectar, and cook for 3 to 4 minutes. Whisk in the coconut cream.

If you're using the homemade pesto, make it now (see details in the recipe Notes).

Place a large skillet or grill pan on medium-high heat. Drizzle 2 slices of bread with a touch of olive oil, but this is optional. It will still toast without the oil. Place the slices oil-side down on the pan. Top with the vegan mozzarella cheese and dollop 2 tablespoons (30 ml) of pesto on top of each. Then place the other slices on top and press down a bit, and cook for 2 to 3 minutes until the bottom slices of bread become golden brown. Then gently flip and cook for 2 to 3 minutes. Serve the sandwiches with the creamy tomato soup.

Notes: Coconut cream is the thicker, more solid part of a can of full-fat coconut milk. You can make sure that it's separate by placing the can in the refrigerator for a few hours prior.

Make an amazing homemade herb pistachio pesto by adding the following to a food processor and blending until smooth: 1½ packed tablespoons (4 g) of fresh basil, ¾ of a medium bunch of fresh dill, 1½ packed tablespoons (5 g) of fresh parsley, ¼ cup (60 ml) of olive oil, 1 large clove of garlic, 2 tablespoons (30 ml) of lemon juice, ¼ to ½ teaspoon of kosher salt, ½ teaspoon of pepper, ¼ cup (31 g) of shelled roasted pistachios, and ½ cup (57 g) of vegan Parmesan shreds (or ⅓ cup [33 g] of grated vegan Parmesan).

Lentil & Mushroom Curry with Spinach & Tomatoes

This Indian-inspired curry is one of my favorites and features amazing spices like coriander, cumin, and curry powder. This isn't a traditionally prepared curry, but it's so delicious and really hits the spot for a comforting meal that you can make quickly and simply. The flavor boosters here, in addition to the spices, are the onion and mushrooms. These combine deliciously with the tomatoes and coconut milk for a hearty, rich sauce. I like to serve this curry with toasted naan and topped with chopped fresh cilantro and red chili flakes.

Servings: 3

1 cup (192 g) dried sprouted lentils (see Note)

2 tsp (10 g) kosher salt, divided

½ large onion

1 tbsp (15 ml) avocado oil

8 oz (226 g) mushrooms

2 cups (298 g) cherry or grape tomatoes

1 tsp chili powder

½ tsp black pepper

1 tbsp (8 g) garlic powder

2½ tsp (5 g) ground coriander

1 tbsp (6 g) curry powder

2 tsp (4 g) ground cumin

¼ cup (60 ml) marinara sauce

1 (15-oz [425-g]) can full-fat coconut milk

1 cup (30 g) baby spinach

2 tbsp (4 g) fresh cilantro

Naan, for serving

Red chili flakes, for serving

To make the lentils, add the lentils, 1 teaspoon of salt, and 3 cups (720 ml) of water to a medium-sized saucepan, cover, and bring it to a boil. Reduce the heat to a gentle simmer and cook the lentils, according to the package directions for al dente. Drain away any remaining liquid.

While the lentils are cooking, finely chop the onion and add it to a large pan on medium-high heat, along with the oil. Stir the onion and let it cook for 1 minute while you slice the mushrooms. Add the mushrooms to the pan, stir, and cook for 3 minutes, stirring halfway. While the mushrooms are cooking, halve the tomatoes.

Reduce the heat to medium and add the tomatoes, remaining 1 teaspoon of salt, chili powder, pepper, garlic powder, ground coriander, curry powder, and cumin, then stir and cook it for 1 minute. Add the marinara sauce and coconut milk, and cook for 2 to 3 minutes, adding in the cooked lentils when they're ready, along with the spinach during the last minute of cooking. Finely chop the cilantro and toast the naan. Serve the curry with the cilantro, red chili flakes, and naan.

Note: If you can't find sprouted lentils, canned lentils can be used. Alternatively, you can cook regular dried lentil varieties like green, red, or black lentils, cooked to al dente, but it will extend the cooking time past 15 minutes. Feel free to cook the lentils a few minutes past al dente for a creamier texture. For the recipe, you're looking for 2⅓ cups (462 g) of cooked lentils.

Smoky Pinto Bean, Mushroom, & Tomato Soup

This Smoky Pinto Bean, Mushroom, & Tomato Soup is brimming with the good stuff. Onion and mushrooms form the base of the soup, then a nice splash of white wine and a variety of dried pantry seasonings add delicious depth of flavor in short order. Pinto beans and collard greens make it so hearty, with a touch of creaminess from a mix of tahini and plant-based plain yogurt. If you don't have collard greens on hand, baby spinach or kale (tough stems removed) would be great substitutes.

Servings: 3 to 4

½ medium yellow onion

1 tbsp (15 ml) olive oil

6 oz (170 ml) cremini or baby portobello mushrooms

1 tsp kosher salt

½ tsp black pepper

2 tsp (3 g) garlic powder

2 tsp (1 g) dried parsley

1 tsp smoked paprika

1 tsp ground cumin

⅓ cup (80 ml) dry white wine

1 (15-oz [425-g]) can pinto beans, drained and rinsed

1 cup (240 g) canned crushed tomatoes

2 cups (480 ml) vegetable broth

1 cup (87 g) frozen collard greens

2 tbsp (30 ml) runny tahini (see Note)

1 tbsp (15 ml) plain, unsweetened almond-based yogurt (optional)

Red chili flakes, for serving (optional)

Preheat a large pot or deep pan on medium-high heat, and finely chop the onion. Add the onion and oil to the pan, and let it cook for 1 to 2 minutes. Meanwhile, slice the mushrooms and stir them in, along with the salt and pepper. Let the vegetables cook for 3 minutes, stirring halfway.

While the vegetables cook, measure out the garlic powder, dried parsley, smoked paprika, and cumin onto a plate. Add the white wine and seasonings to the pan, and let everything cook for 1 to 2 minutes, stirring periodically, as the liquid evaporates.

Add the pinto beans, tomatoes, broth, and collard greens, and bring it to a boil, covered. Remove the lid and cook for 1 to 3 minutes. Remove the pan from the heat and stir in the tahini and yogurt, if desired. Serve topped with red chili flakes for spicy heat, if desired, and garnish with extra dried parsley, if desired.

Note: The recipe calls for "runny tahini." Tahini typically comes as either a thick paste or what I'm referring to as the "runny" kind, where the oil separates at the top and when you stir, it's pourable.

Cozy White Bean & Spinach Soup

This hot and creamy soup is perfect for those days when you crave a warm bowl of goodness that's light and super savory. It's also really versatile to make it as hearty as you want. The recipe uses one can of cannellini beans, but for an even heartier soup, you can increase the amount of beans. The blend of seasonings come through for the win, as it's so flavorful and gives additional depth along with the nutritional yeast for some umami nuttiness. This soup will be a great go-to in the chilly months and even all year long.

Servings: 3 to 4

½ medium red onion
1 tbsp (15 ml) olive oil
2 tbsp (28 g) plant-based butter
1 large carrot
¾ tsp kosher salt
¾ tsp black pepper
2½ tsp (3 g) Italian seasoning
1¼ tsp (4 g) garlic powder
½ tsp dried tarragon
1 (15-oz [425-g]) can cannellini beans
2 tbsp (16 g) all-purpose flour
1 cup (240 ml) oat milk, plain, unsweetened
3 cups (720 ml) vegetable broth
3 tbsp (15 g) nutritional yeast
1 packed cup (30 g) baby spinach
Pita chips, for serving

Preheat a large pot or deep pan over medium-high heat. Finely chop the red onion and add it to the pot with the olive oil and butter. Stir and let the onion cook for around 2 minutes. Meanwhile, peel the carrot, trim off the ends, and slice it in half crosswise. Then cut each piece lengthwise into thirds. Make crosswise cuts to thinly slice the carrot. Add the carrot, salt, and pepper to the pot and stir, then reduce the heat to medium. Cover the pot and let the vegetables cook for 4 to 6 minutes, stirring occasionally.

While the vegetables are cooking, measure out the Italian seasoning, garlic powder, and dried tarragon onto a plate, and drain and rinse the cannellini beans.

Stir the flour into the vegetables until they're coated. Gradually pour in the oat milk, stirring as you pour. Add the vegetable broth, seasonings, beans, and nutritional yeast. Cover and bring to a boil, then lower the heat to a simmer and stir in the baby spinach to wilt. Serve topped with pita chips.

Vibrant & Nourishing Bowls

When I think of bowls, I think of flavor and convenience. Just throw everything into a bowl, mix it up, and thoroughly enjoy. No fussing needed, just fresh and bold ingredients. And these recipes will certainly deliver on that! Many of the recipes in this chapter also have a variety of ingredients, which tends to be another calling card of the alluring "bowl." Yet they're still super fast! Some perfect examples are the light-yet-satisfying Rice Noodle & Kale Bowl with Ginger Almond Butter Dressing (page 104), and the Arugula Pasta Bowl with Garlic Croutons & Herb Vinaigrette (page 108). And for some amazing warming flavors, I turn to the delicious Indian-Inspired Veggie Bowl with Yogurt Sauce (page 115).

This chapter is packed with varieties of flavor profiles too. So whether you're in the mood for Asian-inspired flavors of smoky tofu and quick-pickled cucumbers with jasmine rice and spicy vegan mayo, or Mediterranean-inspired toasted pearl couscous with hearty chickpeas, lemon, and herbs, this chapter has you covered!

Pearl Couscous Bowl with Roasted Red Peppers, Artichokes, & Chickpeas

This pearl couscous bowl is an example of simple ingredients coming together to make something super delicious. I'm obsessed with this yogurt sauce, and it's so delicious in combination with the seasoned pearl couscous and other goods in this bowl—like roasted red peppers, marinated artichokes, chickpeas, and slivered almonds for crunch. I love to serve this bowl with crisp pita chips. For the salad greens, here we use a mix of leafy greens. This bowl would also be great with arugula or even kale. Simply massage the kale leaves with a touch of olive oil or lemon juice to soften the leaves.

Servings: 2 to 3

2 tsp (10 ml) olive oil

1 cup (173 g) dry pearl couscous (see Notes)

1¼ cups (300 ml) vegetable broth

1 tbsp (15 ml) runny tahini (see Notes)

2 tbsp (30 ml) lemon juice (about 1 lemon), divided

⅓ cup (80 ml) plain, unsweetened almond-based yogurt

1 tsp dried drill or 1 tbsp (3 g) fresh dill, finely chopped

¾ tsp kosher salt, divided

¾ tsp garlic powder, divided

2 tsp (10 ml) agave nectar (optional)

½ cup (160 g) roasted red peppers, drained

½ cup (84 g) marinated artichoke hearts, drained

½ cup (52 g) cucumber, sliced

1 cup (164 g) canned chickpeas, drained and rinsed

2–3 servings salad greens

2 tbsp (14 g) slivered almonds (optional)

1 cup (50 g) pita chips (optional)

⅓ cup (50 g) vegan feta (optional)

To make the pearl couscous, add the olive oil and pearl couscous to a small saucepan, stir, and place it over medium heat, covered. Allow the pan to heat up for 1 to 2 minutes, then add the vegetable broth and bring it to a boil, covered. Turn the heat to a low simmer and cook the couscous for approximately 6 minutes, until all of the broth is absorbed.

Meanwhile, prepare the yogurt sauce. To a small bowl, add the tahini, half of the lemon juice, yogurt, dill, ½ teaspoon of salt, ½ teaspoon of garlic powder, and agave to a bowl, and mix them together well. Next, give the roasted red peppers and marinated artichokes a coarse chop, and dice the cucumber.

When the couscous has cooked, stir in the remaining lemon juice, remaining ¼ teaspoon of salt, remaining ¼ teaspoon of garlic powder, and chickpeas. Serve by dividing the salad greens into bowls, and top the greens with the roasted red peppers, artichokes, cucumbers, couscous–chickpea mixture, and the almonds and pita chips, if desired. Top with the tahini yogurt sauce and vegan feta, if desired.

Notes: If you're up for it, toast the pearl couscous before cooking to add extra flavor. Allow the pearl couscous to get light golden brown in color as it heats in the oil, before adding the vegetable broth. Stir the pearl couscous every 20 to 30 seconds to ensure even toasting.

The recipe calls for "runny tahini." Tahini typically comes as either a thick paste or what I'm referring to as the "runny" kind, where the oil separates at the top and when you stir, it's pourable.

Rice Noodle & Kale Bowl with Ginger Almond Butter Dressing

This bowl is a colorful and texture-filled combination of noodles, carrot, crunchy roasted peanuts, and nutrient-rich kale that's dressed in the yummiest Asian-inspired almond butter dressing. Hints of lemon, ginger, and sesame also help to flavor the dressing, and you may find a lot of other tasty uses for this sauce besides this bowl. It makes a fantastic salad dressing or dipping sauce too. The edamame provides delicious flavor and texture, plus plant protein. The fresh mint rounds out the dish with that dreamy aroma and taste that only fresh mint can give. But if you don't have fresh mint on hand, no worries! Fresh cilantro or basil would be great alternatives.

Servings: 3 to 4

Noodle and Kale Bowl

7 oz (198 g) rice noodle linguini

2 tsp (10 ml) toasted sesame oil, divided

¾ cup (93 g) shelled edamame

¾ medium bunch kale

Juice of ½ lemon

Pinch of kosher salt and black pepper

1 large carrot

⅓ cup (49 g) roasted peanuts

3 large fresh mint leaves

Dressing (see Note)

2 tbsp (32 g) almond butter

2 tbsp (32 g) ginger paste

1 tbsp (15 ml) agave nectar

1 tbsp (15 ml) toasted sesame oil

1 tbsp (15 ml) reduced-sodium soy sauce

1 tbsp (15 ml) rice vinegar

2–3 tsp (10–15 ml) chili garlic sauce, to taste

1 tbsp (15 ml) water, to thin

3 large fresh mint leaves

To make the rice noodles, fill a large pot with 2 inches (5 cm) of water, enough to fully submerge the noodles, cover, and bring it to a boil. Once boiling, add the rice noodles. Stir and cook the noodles according to the package directions for al dente, and rinse them after draining. Drizzle 1 teaspoon of the toasted sesame oil on the drained noodles, and toss.

If your edamame is frozen, add them to a small bowl and cover them with water to thaw. Drain them prior to serving. To prepare the kale, cut out the tough stems and thinly slice them into bite-sized pieces. Pat the leaves dry and place them into a large bowl. Drizzle the kale with the remaining 1 teaspoon of toasted sesame oil and lemon juice with a pinch of salt and pepper. Massage the kale leaves with your fingers to soften them.

For the dressing, to a small bowl, add the almond butter, ginger paste, agave nectar, sesame oil, soy sauce, rice vinegar, and chili garlic sauce, and whisk thoroughly. Slowly whisk in some water to thin, if needed. Grate or thinly slice the carrot, and give the roasted peanuts a coarse chop. Also, thinly slice all six of the mint leaves; add half of the mint into the dressing.

To serve, divide the noodles and kale leaves between your bowls. Then top the bowls with the carrot, peanuts, edamame, and remaining sliced mint. Serve it with the Ginger Almond Butter Dressing.

Note: If you would like to make the dressing a bit less almond buttery, try adding 1 tablespoon (15 ml) of tahini into the dressing and another tablespoon (15 ml) of water.

Veggie Fajita Bowl with Fresh Salsa & Avocado

In this Veggie Fajita Bowl with Fresh Salsa & Avocado, there's so much goodness in one place! The bowl consists of seasoned pinto beans and onion as the fajita "filling," plus avocado, fresh chunky salsa, and blue corn chips. This recipe is a great candidate for doubling the recipe to feed a larger number of people; just keep in mind that the time will increase somewhat due to the extra prep time. It's a fun recipe for people to customize their own bowls. In addition to serving with lime wedges, you can also serve these with hot sauce and/or vegan sour cream. It's a great base recipe to get creative!

Servings: 2 to 3

Fajita Bowl

½ red onion

2 tbsp (30 ml) olive oil

1 bell pepper

1 tsp kosher salt

1 tsp chili powder

1 tsp garlic powder

1 tsp cumin

1 tsp oregano

1 (15-oz [425-g]) can pinto beans, drained and rinsed

1 avocado

Pinch of black pepper

2–3 oz (56–84 g) blue corn tortilla chips, for serving

Finely chopped cilantro, for serving

Lime wedges, for serving (optional)

Simple Tomato Salsa

1 large tomato

½ tbsp (8 ml) lime juice (about ¼ lime)

1 tsp olive oil

Pinch of kosher salt, black pepper, and garlic powder

¼–½ jalapeño, finely chopped (optional)

Preheat a large pan over medium heat. Slice the onion and add it to the pan, along with the olive oil. Stir and let it cook while you slice the bell pepper. Add the bell pepper to the pan, stir, and cook it for 3 to 4 minutes. Then add the salt, chili powder, garlic powder, cumin, oregano, and pinto beans. Stir and cook for 1 to 2 minutes.

Meanwhile, prepare the salsa. Dice the tomato and add it to a small bowl, along with the lime juice, olive oil, salt, pepper, garlic powder, and jalapeño, if using. Mash the avocado and add a pinch of salt, pepper, and garlic powder to the mashed avocado.

To serve, divide the beans and vegetable mixture between your bowls, and top them with the salsa, mashed avocado, blue corn tortilla chips, and cilantro. Serve it with lime wedges, if desired.

Arugula Pasta Bowl with Garlic Croutons & Herb Vinaigrette

This bowl is everything I want in a light, savory meal: bold flavors from the dressing, crispy yet chewy crouton heaven, and a great blend of carbs, proteins, and veggies (although I love a good straight-up pasta meal, too, as you may already know!). You can use your pasta of choice; just make sure you do not overcook it, as we really need it to hold its shape in this type of dish. For quick homemade croutons, I try to find a fresh-baked/bakery whole grain or multigrain, seedy bread to get extra nutrients if possible. The bread will toast up into yummy croutons that we flavor with garlic powder.

Servings: 3 to 4

2¼ tsp (12 g) kosher salt, divided

1 cup (75 g) uncooked whole wheat rotini

5 tbsp (75 ml) olive oil, divided

9 oz (250 g) whole wheat bread loaf, unsliced

¾ tsp black pepper, divided

½ tsp garlic powder, divided

¼ small red onion

1 cup (149 g) cherry or grape tomatoes

1½ tsp (8 ml) Dijon mustard

1½ tbsp (23 ml) white wine vinegar

1 tbsp (3 g) fresh dill, finely chopped

1 tbsp (4 g) fresh parsley, finely chopped

2.5 oz (71 g) arugula

1 cup (164 g) canned chickpeas, drained and rinsed

1 tbsp (15 ml) lemon juice (about ½ lemon; optional)

To make the pasta, fill a medium saucepan with 2 inches (5 cm) of water, enough to fully submerge the pasta, cover, and bring it to a boil. Add 1 teaspoon of salt and the dry pasta, stir, and cover to bring to a boil again. Then uncover the pan and cook the pasta according to the package directions for al dente. Drain the pasta in a colander and run the colander under cool water for 10 to 20 seconds to cool down the pasta.

Meanwhile, prepare the croutons. Preheat a large pan on medium heat with 2 tablespoons (30 ml) of the olive oil. Cut the bread into 1-inch (2.5-cm) cubes, add it to the pan, and toss. Sprinkle in ¼ teaspoon each of the salt, pepper, and garlic powder. Cook the croutons for 10 to 12 minutes until they are crisp, stirring periodically, and sprinkling in another ¼ teaspoon of garlic powder halfway through cooking.

While the croutons are cooking, thinly slice the red onion and halve the tomatoes. In a small bowl, make the dressing by whisking together the remaining 3 tablespoons (45 ml) of olive oil, mustard, white wine vinegar, fresh dill, parsley, and the remaining 1 teaspoon of salt and ½ teaspoon of pepper.

To assemble, arrange the arugula in bowls and top them with the onion, tomatoes, chickpeas, pasta, and croutons. Drizzle the dressing over the top, to taste, as well as the lemon juice, if using.

Orange Ginger Chickpeas & Peppers

This cozy dish is a sweet and spicy combination of delicious veggies and chickpeas that is ready in a flash. It has bold orange, ginger, and lime flavors, and is topped with sesame seeds and chives. This one ticks all the boxes for flavor and heartiness, plus it's filled with vibrant and nourishing ingredients. The bell peppers make a perfect sweet pair for the chickpeas and orange in the recipe, and they also allow you to get your veggies in at the same time. You can easily increase or decrease the spicy heat in this recipe by adjusting the amount of the chili garlic sauce.

Servings: 3

Chickpeas and Peppers
1 cup (200 g) jasmine rice

1½ bell peppers

1 tbsp (15 ml) toasted sesame oil

Pinch of kosher salt and black pepper

2 large cloves garlic

1 (15-oz [425-g]) can chickpeas, drained and rinsed

2 tbsp (6 g) fresh or dried chives

2 tsp (6 g) sesame seeds

Sauce
1 tbsp (8 g) cornstarch

2 tbsp (30 ml) water

¾ cups (180 ml) orange juice

2 tsp (10 ml) chili garlic sauce

1 tsp hoisin sauce

1 tbsp (15 ml) lime juice (½–¾ lime)

2 tbsp (30 ml) soy sauce (see Note)

2 tsp (10 ml) toasted sesame oil

1 tbsp (16 g) ginger paste

1½ tbsp (23 ml) maple syrup

In a medium saucepan, add the jasmine rice plus 2 cups (480 ml) of water. Cover and bring to a boil, then immediately reduce the heat to low and cook until the rice is tender and the water has been absorbed, around 12 minutes.

Meanwhile, preheat a large pan over medium-high heat. Dice the bell peppers and add them to the pan with the toasted sesame oil. Season the bell peppers with a pinch of salt and pepper, stir, and let them cook for 6 to 7 minutes on medium to medium-high heat, stirring periodically.

While the bell peppers are cooking, make the sauce by whisking together the cornstarch and water in a bowl, followed by the orange juice, chili garlic sauce, hoisin sauce, lime juice, soy sauce, sesame oil, ginger paste, and maple syrup.

Mince the garlic, then add the garlic, chickpeas, and sauce to the pan with the bell peppers.

Stir, cover, and cook at a gentle simmer for 2 to 4 minutes, stirring occasionally. While these are cooking, chop the chives. Serve with the cooked rice, and top with chopped chives and sesame seeds.

Note: For more saltiness in the dish, stir in an additional teaspoon of soy sauce.

Smoky Tofu Bowl with Spicy Mayo

This Smoky Tofu Bowl with Spicy Mayo is a delicious and simple bowl filled with flavor and nourishing ingredients. I like using super-firm tofu here, as it holds its texture very well when tossed in the dreamy sauce and topped with the spicy Asian-inspired mayo. Feel free to halve the amount of chili garlic sauce if you prefer a little less spice. The sliced cucumber and bright cilantro add a wonderful freshness and vibrancy to the dish. If you have some extra time, you can do a quick pickle of your cucumbers using the method on page 55.

Servings: 3 to 4

Tofu Bowl
1 cup (200 g) jasmine rice
16 oz (454 g) super-firm tofu
½ tbsp (8 ml) toasted sesame oil
Pinch of kosher salt and black pepper
½ medium seedless cucumber
¾ cup (93 g) shelled edamame (see Note)
Sesame seeds, for serving
3 tbsp (8 g) thinly sliced scallions
Cilantro, for serving

Spicy Mayo
¼ cup (60 ml) vegan mayo
½ tsp soy sauce
1 tsp sesame oil
½ tsp ground ginger
¼ tsp garlic powder
1½ tsp (8 ml) rice vinegar
½ tbsp (8 ml) chili garlic sauce

Tofu Sauce
2 tbsp (30 ml) soy sauce
1 tbsp (15 ml) rice vinegar
2 tbsp (30 ml) maple syrup
½ tsp garlic powder
¼ tsp ground ginger

In a medium saucepan, add the jasmine rice plus 2 cups (480 ml) of water. Bring it to a boil, covered, then immediately reduce the heat to low and cook until the rice is tender and the water has evaporated, around 12 minutes.

Meanwhile, preheat a large pan over medium-high heat. Drain the tofu and pat it dry. Slice it into cubes, around ½ inch (1.3 cm) in size, and add them to the pan along with the toasted sesame oil. Sprinkle the tofu with a pinch of salt and pepper. Cook the tofu for 8 to 10 minutes, turning every few minutes to brown on several sides.

While the tofu is cooking, make the Spicy Mayo. In a small bowl, whisk together the mayo, soy sauce, sesame oil, ground ginger, garlic powder, rice vinegar, and chili garlic sauce.

Make the Tofu Sauce. In a small bowl, whisk together the soy sauce, rice vinegar, maple syrup, garlic powder, and ground ginger.

During the last 2 minutes of the tofu cooking, add in the Tofu Sauce, toss, and cook for 2 minutes. The tofu will absorb most of the sauce during this time.

Thinly slice the seedless cucumber. Serve the tofu with the rice, cucumber, edamame, sesame seeds, scallions, and cilantro. Drizzle it with the Spicy Mayo.

Note: If your edamame is frozen, add the edamame to a small bowl with warm water to thaw while you prepare the dish, then drain prior to serving.

Indian-Inspired Veggie Bowl with Yogurt Sauce

This meal, and those very similar to it, are special to me because they were the first meals I cooked for my husband on my plant-based journey. This yummy meal is hearty and satisfying from the mix of broccoli and black beans, with corn for some sweetness. I love the cilantro-lemon yogurt sauce, too, as it makes such a perfect accompaniment for the seasonings in this bowl.

Servings: 3 to 4

Veggie Bowl

8 oz (226 g) broccoli florets (see Note)

2 tbsp (30 ml) olive or avocado oil, plus more for naan (optional)

¼ cup (60 ml) filtered water

1 tsp kosher salt

1 tsp cumin

1 tsp chili powder

1 tsp garlic powder, plus more for naan (optional)

1 tsp curry powder

1 cup (136 g) frozen corn

1 (15-oz [425-g]) can black beans, drained and rinsed

3–4 servings naan

Finely chopped cilantro, for naan (optional)

Yogurt Sauce

1 packed tbsp (1 g) fresh cilantro, plus extra for serving

5 oz (148 ml) plain, unsweetened almond-based yogurt

½ tsp kosher salt

½ tsp black pepper

½ tsp garlic powder

Juice of ¾ lemon

In a large pan on medium-high heat, add the broccoli florets, oil, and water, then bring it to a boil, covered. Reduce the heat to medium and add the salt, cumin, chili powder, garlic powder, curry powder, corn, and black beans. Stir, cover again, and let the mixture continue to cook for 6 to 9 minutes, stirring occasionally, until the broccoli is fork tender. Some browning on the vegetables is fine.

While the vegetables are cooking, prepare the Yogurt Sauce. Finely chop the fresh cilantro. In a small bowl, add the yogurt, salt, pepper, garlic powder, and lemon juice. Add in the chopped cilantro, and stir well. Toast the naan, and if you'd like to jazz it up, drizzle the naan with a touch of olive oil, garlic powder, and finely chopped fresh cilantro.

To serve, divide the vegetable mixture between the bowls and top the veggies with the Yogurt Sauce. Serve it with the toasted naan.

Note: As an alternative to fresh broccoli, you can use a 12-ounce (336-g) bag of frozen broccoli. While the cook time will remain the same, I suggest removing the cover on the pan for the last 3 to 4 minutes of cooking, to allow any remaining liquid to evaporate.

Black Beans with Rice, Avocado, & Fresh Salsa

Get ready for some coziness and amazing textures and flavors! These Black Beans with Rice, Avocado, & Fresh Salsa are a go-to in my house because they're so simple and satisfying. This dish is a perfect mix of fun and variety, with lots of bright colors and tasty fixins. Make yourself a plate of black beans with rice, fresh salsa, tortilla chips, and avocado, and don't forget the cilantro and lime wedges!

Servings: 4

1 cup (200 g) jasmine rice

½ large yellow onion

2 tbsp + 1 tsp (35 ml) olive oil, divided

1¼ tsp (7 g) kosher salt, divided

1½ cups (224 g) cherry or grape tomatoes

¼ tsp black pepper

1¼ tsp (4 g) garlic powder, divided

2 limes, divided

1 tsp dried oregano

1 tsp onion powder

¼ tsp smoked paprika

1 tsp cumin

2 (15-oz [425-g]) cans black beans

½ cup (120 ml) store-bought or homemade marinara sauce

2 tbsp (30 ml) full-fat coconut milk or plain, unsweetened almond-based yogurt (see Note)

2 tbsp (2 g) cilantro, plus more for serving

1 avocado

4 servings blue corn tortilla chips, for serving

In a medium saucepan, add the jasmine rice plus 2 cups (480 ml) of water. Bring it to a boil, covered, then immediately reduce the heat to low, and cook the rice until it is tender and the water has evaporated, around 12 minutes.

Meanwhile, preheat a large pan on medium-high heat. Finely chop the onion and add it to the pan with 2 tablespoons (30 ml) of the oil and 1 teaspoon of salt. Reduce the heat to medium, stir, and let it cook for 5 to 6 minutes, stirring periodically.

While the onion is cooking, prepare the tomatoes for the salsa. Chop the tomatoes and add them to a medium bowl, keeping as much of the tomato juice as possible, with ¼ teaspoon each of the salt, pepper, and garlic powder. Add the remaining 1 teaspoon of olive oil and juice of ¼ of a lime unless your lime is dry, in which case use ½ of a lime. Stir everything together.

To the pan with the onion, add the remaining 1 teaspoon of garlic powder, dried oregano, onion powder, smoked paprika, and cumin, and stir. Drain and rinse the black beans and add them to the pan, along with the marinara and coconut milk. Stir it and continue to cook the beans on medium-low heat, covered, while you finely chop the cilantro, slice the avocado, and cut the remaining limes into wedges. Serve the beans with the rice, salsa, cilantro, avocado, tortilla chips, and lime wedges.

Note: Both the coconut milk and yogurt work great in this dish. The yogurt will make it creamier, almost like a vegan sour cream vibe. If you are using the coconut milk and wondering what to do with the rest of the can, I've got you covered! Use the rest to make Sun-Dried Tomato Alfredo Penne with Broccoli (page 30), Creamy Mushroom, Chickpea, & Sun-Dried Tomato Soup (page 90), or Creamy Carrot, Zucchini, & Olive Pasta (page 33).

Buffalo Tempeh & Avocado Bowl with Vegan Honey Mustard

Spicy meets sweet in this simple and really flavorful tempeh bowl. The red cabbage and romaine provide a perfect crisp contrast to the creamy avocado and savory, spicy tempeh. I love the sweetness that the Vegan Honey Mustard brings, to pair with the other flavors. Make sure to get your tempeh nice and crispy before adding in the hot sauce. And if you're not a big fan of hot sauce, you can substitute BBQ sauce!

Servings: 2

Tempeh & Avocado Bowl
1 tbsp (15 ml) avocado oil

7 oz (198 g) tempeh

½ small yellow onion

Pinch of kosher salt and black pepper

2–3 tbsp (30–45 ml) hot sauce (such as Frank's RedHot)

1 avocado

2 servings romaine lettuce, dried well

½ cup (35 g) thinly sliced red cabbage

Vegan Honey Mustard
¼ cup (60 ml) vegan mayo

4 tsp (20 ml) Dijon mustard

2 tbsp (30 ml) agave nectar

¼ tsp kosher salt

¼ tsp garlic powder

To make the tempeh, preheat a pan on medium-high heat and add the avocado oil. Slice the tempeh block crosswise in the center, then make three lengthwise cuts to create eight strips total. Add the tempeh strips to the pan and let them cook for 1 to 2 minutes. Thinly slice the onion and add it to the pan in the gaps between the tempeh, and lower the heat to medium. Season the tempeh and onion with a pinch of salt and pepper, and cook for 4 to 6 minutes, flipping halfway. You are looking for crispness and browning on the tempeh, and some browning on the onion is good too.

While the tempeh is cooking, prepare the Vegan Honey Mustard. To a small bowl, add the mayo, mustard, agave nectar, salt, and garlic powder. Whisk them together.

When the tempeh is finished cooking, drizzle in the hot sauce and gently toss the tempeh, being careful not to break up the strips. Slice the avocado and chop the romaine lettuce.

To serve, add the romaine, red cabbage, tempeh–onion mixture, and avocado to bowls and top them with the Vegan Honey Mustard as desired.

Note: The dressing recipe makes a bit extra than you may need for this recipe, so you can save any remainder in the fridge for up to 3 days.

Southwest Scramble-for-Dinner Bowl

This is one of those meals that hits the spot every time, no matter what meal it is! Dinner, lunch, or break-fast, this yummy bowl has your back. You can get creative with the fixins too. For example, you can use bell peppers if you prefer those over roasted red peppers. Black beans would be delicious in here, too, as well as roasted vegetables that you may have as leftovers from the fridge. You can also serve this scramble as a wrap or even as a topping for nachos!

Servings: 2 to 3

14 oz (396 g) extra-firm tofu

2 tsp (10 ml) avocado oil, divided

¼ tsp turmeric

½ tsp kosher salt, divided

½ tsp black pepper, divided

½ tsp garlic powder, divided

1 small yellow onion

¼ tsp chili powder

½ cup (68 g) frozen corn

¼ cup (80 g) roasted red peppers, drained

1 avocado

⅓ cup (80 ml) salsa, store-bought or homemade (from the Veggie Fajita Bowl with Fresh Salsa & Avocado recipe [page 107])

1–2 tbsp (9–19 g) crumbled vegan feta (optional)

Arugula, sliced tomato, and lime wedges, for serving (optional)

Place a large pan on medium-high heat. Drain the tofu and gently squeeze out extra water with your hands. Crumble the tofu into the pan, leaving some chunks larger than others for texture, similar to chunky scrambled eggs. Add 1 teaspoon of the avocado oil, the turmeric, ¼ teaspoon of salt, ¼ teaspoon of pepper, and ¼ teaspoon of garlic powder. Gently stir the tofu to incorporate the seasonings. Reduce the heat to medium and cook the tofu for 5 to 8 minutes, stirring occasionally, until your desired firmness.

While the tofu is cooking, preheat a second pan on medium-high heat and add the remaining 1 teaspoon of avocado oil. Finely chop the onion and add it to the pan, along with the remaining ¼ teaspoon of salt, ¼ teaspoon of pepper, ¼ teaspoon of garlic powder, and the chili powder. Reduce the heat to medium-low and cook the onion for 3 minutes, then add the frozen corn and cook for 2 minutes.

Meanwhile, chop the roasted red peppers and dice or slice the avocado. Gently fold the onion–corn mixture and the roasted peppers into the tofu. Top the tofu scramble with the avocado, salsa, and optional vegan feta. Serve with arugula, tomato, and lime wedges, if desired.

Quick & Flavorful Stir-Fries & Sautés

Stir-fries and cozy, sautéed plates are some of my favorite dinners. They tend to pack a flavor punch, and the possibilities are endless when it comes to ingredient combinations. From chickpeas, vegan sausage, and tofu for our proteins to mushrooms, peppers, Brussels sprouts, and zucchini for our veggies—there's lots to love in this chapter.

For many of the Asian-inspired meals, we use ingredients like mirin, gochujang, and hoisin sauce. These sauces will provide big flavor in a short amount of time. We'll also use relatively high heat to get our tofu crisp for some recipes and to achieve deliciously browned mushrooms. Several recipes call for super-firm tofu, as this firmness will help the crisping process in such a short amount of time. Alternatively, you can press extra-firm tofu for 20 to 30 minutes prior to cooking, to remove excess water and firm it up.

Cozy up with Spiced Chickpeas and Zucchini with Herb Lentils (page 133) or Udon Noodles with Mushrooms, Tofu, & Green Beans (page 134) on a chilly evening for a satisfying meal that will make you happy you chose to make dinner at home. Or get spicy with Spicy Gochujang Tofu & Asparagus Stir-Fry (page 137), which has a nice kick of heat and crisp-tender, pan-fried asparagus.

Warm Mediterranean Couscous & Veggies

This warm and cozy meal is something I could eat all year round. The recipe is Mediterranean inspired, with a touch of sumac seasoning for additional depth of flavor in a short amount of time. You'll find sumac prevalent in Middle Eastern cooking, and if you haven't used it before, you may find yourself obsessed like I was the first time I tried it! This dish is light, super comforting from the warm vegetables and chickpeas, and full of citrusy, herby flavors. The tomatoes give a great burst of freshness, and the green olives and vegan feta are additions that make the dish feel extra special. If green olives aren't your thing, Kalamata olives or capers would be amazing in here. Alternatively, you can leave them out and add an extra squeeze of lemon to the dish.

Servings: 3 to 4

1 cup (173 g) dry couscous

1¼ tsp (5 g) kosher salt, divided

1 tsp garlic powder, divided

2 tbsp (30 ml) olive oil, divided

2 tbsp (30 ml) lemon juice (about 1 lemon)

¼ red onion

2 bell peppers

1 cup (149 g) cherry or grape tomatoes

¼ cup (57 g) sliced sun-dried tomatoes packed in oil, drained

1 (15-oz [425-g]) can chickpeas, drained and rinsed

¾ tsp sumac

½ tsp black pepper

2 packed tbsp (8 g) fresh parsley

⅓ cup (59 g) pitted green olives

⅓ cup (50 g) vegan feta (optional)

To make the couscous, add 1 cup (240 ml) of water to a small saucepan and bring it to a boil, covered. Add the couscous, ½ teaspoon of salt, and ½ teaspoon of garlic powder. Turn off the heat, give it a quick stir, then cover and let it sit for 5 minutes. Add in 1 tablespoon (15 ml) of the olive oil and the lemon juice, and stir to fluff the couscous.

Meanwhile, heat a large pan over medium-high heat. Finely chop the red onion and add it to the pan with the remaining 1 tablespoon (15 ml) of olive oil. Stir the onion and let it cook for 3 to 4 minutes while preparing the bell peppers.

Dice the bell peppers small, then add them to the pan. Stir and let them cook for 1 to 2 minutes on medium heat, partially covered, while halving the cherry tomatoes. Some browning is good. Add the tomatoes, sun-dried tomatoes, chickpeas, sumac, remaining ¾ teaspoon of salt, pepper, and remaining ½ teaspoon of garlic powder. Stir everything together and cook for 3 to 4 minutes on medium heat, covered, or until the bell peppers are tender.

To finish up the dish, finely chop the fresh parsley and stir half of it into the couscous and half into the vegetable–chickpea mixture. Serve the vegetable–chickpea mixture on top of the couscous, and top it with the green olives and optional vegan feta.

Spicy, Sweet, & Sour Tofu Broccoli Stir-Fry

There's not much better than grabbing your fork and getting up close and personal with a satisfying plate of this tofu and broccoli. The combination of spicy, sweet, and sour makes this dish so inviting. This recipe has a bit more multitasking going on with the rice, broccoli, and tofu going at the same time, followed by the sauce. So if you'd like to save cleanup for one of the pans, feel free to cook the sauce in the same pan you used to steam the broccoli in beforehand. Alternatively, you can steam the broccoli in the microwave. If you're not in the mood for a cornstarch coating on the tofu, feel free to forego that step altogether and let the tofu pan-fry as-is.

Servings: 3 to 4

Stir-Fry

1 cup (200 g) jasmine rice

10 oz (283 g) precut broccoli florets, bite-sized pieces

½ cup (64 g) cornstarch

¼ cup (60 ml) avocado oil

16 oz (454 g) super-firm tofu

¼ tsp kosher salt

¼ tsp black pepper

¼ large red onion

2 tsp (6 g) sesame seeds, for serving

3 tbsp (8 g) sliced scallions, for serving

Sauce

¼ cup (60 ml) ketchup

2½ tbsp (38 ml) agave nectar

2 tsp (10 ml) soy sauce

2 tbsp (30 ml) gochujang

1½ tbsp (23 ml) rice vinegar

¼ cup (60 ml) orange juice

1 tsp garlic powder

1 tsp chili garlic sauce

In a medium saucepan, add the jasmine rice plus 2 cups (480 ml) of water. Bring it to a boil, covered, then immediately reduce the heat to low and cook it until the rice is tender and the water has been absorbed, around 12 minutes.

To prepare the broccoli, add the florets and approximately 1 inch (2.5 cm) of water to a medium saucepan and bring it to a boil, covered. Reduce the heat to low and cook for 3 to 4 minutes, or until it's crisp-tender, then drain the broccoli and set it aside.

Meanwhile, add the cornstarch to a large mixing bowl. Preheat a large pan on medium-high heat and add the oil. Let the oil heat up while you drain the tofu and cut it into ½-inch (1.3-cm) cubes. Toss the tofu cubes in the cornstarch to coat, then transfer the tofu to the pan, gently shaking off any excess cornstarch. Be careful to avoid oil splatter. Season the tofu with salt and pepper, and cook for 7 to 9 minutes, until it's lightly golden, gently tossing every few minutes. While the tofu cooks, slice or chop the onion and add it to the pan to cook with the tofu.

While the tofu cooks, make the sauce. To a small saucepan, add the ketchup and agave nectar, and begin cooking on medium to medium-high heat as you add the soy sauce, gochujang, rice vinegar, orange juice, garlic powder, and chili garlic sauce, stirring together until smooth. Once it simmers and thickens somewhat, add it to the crispy tofu, along with the cooked broccoli. Gently stir together and serve with the rice, sesame seeds, and scallions.

Brussels Sprouts with Saucy Tofu

This dish is saucy, comforting, and filled with satisfying tofu and vegetables. Served with rice, it makes a complete meal that is not only hearty but also super quick to make! The flavors here are really simple, where the sliced tofu soaks up the delicious brothy sauce during the cooking process. The tofu also gets amazing flavor from the Brussels sprouts and onion cooking beside it. It all comes together in a warm and cozy meal, topped with sliced scallions and extra chili sauce, if you wish, for more spicy heat.

Servings: 3

Brussels Sprouts and Tofu
1 cup (200 g) jasmine rice
½ lb (226 g) prehalved Brussels sprouts
2 tbsp (30 ml) toasted sesame oil, divided
¼ large red onion
12 oz (336 g) super-firm tofu
Scallions, for serving

Sauce
¼ cup (60 ml) tamari
½ tbsp (8 ml) toasted sesame oil
1 tbsp (15 ml) rice vinegar
2 tbsp (30 ml) agave nectar
1–1½ tbsp (15–23 ml) chili garlic sauce or sambal oelek
2 tbsp (30 ml) water
¼ tsp garlic powder

In a medium saucepan, add the jasmine rice plus 2 cups (480 ml) of water. Bring it to a boil, covered, then immediately reduce the heat to low and cook it until the rice is tender and the water has been absorbed, around 12 minutes.

To make the vegetables, preheat a medium pan on medium-high heat. Slice the halved Brussels sprouts in half, through the stem. Add them to the skillet with 1 tablespoon (15 ml) of the toasted sesame oil. Stir and let them cook for 1 to 2 minutes while thinly slicing the red onion. Add the onion to the pan and stir. You'll leave these to cook for 5 to 6 minutes, stirring periodically, and in the meantime start the tofu.

Preheat a large pan on medium-high heat. Cut the tofu lengthwise down the center, then cut crosswise ½ inch (1.3 cm) thick. Add the remaining 1 tablespoon (15 ml) of oil to the pan, and lay out the tofu pieces. Cook for 4 to 5 minutes while preparing the sauce.

For the sauce, in a small bowl, combine the tamari, sesame oil, rice vinegar, agave nectar, chili garlic sauce, water, and garlic powder.

Carefully flip the tofu, then add the Brussels sprouts and onion over top of the tofu. Pour the sauce over everything, and cook it for 2 to 4 minutes as the liquid simmers and thickens somewhat. While the tofu is cooking, thinly slice the scallions. Serve the tofu and vegetables with the jasmine rice, and top it with the scallions.

Vegan Sausage, Peppers, & Spinach with Pearl Couscous

This dish is a twist on the traditional preparation for a childhood favorite of mine. Growing up where I did, there's lots of casual restaurants and pizzerias that serve sausage and peppers. In this vegan version, we use plant-based sausages and flavorful seasonings like cumin and za'atar as an alternative to the Italian American preparation. Choose your favorite sausages, as they'll be the star of the show in this dish. But coming in a close second are the deliciously spiced vegetables like bell pepper and spinach, along with the warm and flavorful pearl couscous. The lemon juice gives a great citrusy brightness to the dish.

Servings: 2 to 4

1 cup (173 g) dry pearl couscous (see Note)

1 tbsp + 1 tsp (20 ml) olive oil, divided

1¼ cups (300 ml) vegetable broth

¼ tsp onion powder

1 bell pepper

½ tsp kosher salt

½ tsp black pepper

4 (3.5-oz [99-g]) vegan sausages (thawed if frozen)

1 tsp garlic powder

½ tsp cumin

2 tsp (1 g) dried parsley

2 tsp (3 g) za'atar seasoning

2 tbsp (3 g) fresh parsley

3 cups (90 g) baby spinach

½ tbsp (8 ml) lemon juice (about ¼ lemon; optional)

To make the pearl couscous, place a small saucepan over medium heat. Add the pearl couscous and 1 teaspoon of the olive oil to the pan. Toast the couscous to a light golden brown, stirring periodically. Stir in the broth and onion powder, cover, and bring it to a boil. Then turn the heat to low and cook, covered, for 5 to 6 minutes, until all the broth is absorbed. Then give it a stir and let it sit, partially covered.

Meanwhile, preheat a large pan on medium heat. Thinly slice the bell pepper and add it to the pan along with the remaining 1 tablespoon (15 ml) of olive oil, salt, and pepper. Stir the bell pepper and let it cook for 1 to 2 minutes while preparing the vegan sausages.

Slice the vegan sausages around ½ inch (1.3 cm) thick. Add them to the pan, nestling them in to allow for contact with the bottom of the pan, and cook for around 3 minutes. While the sausages cook, measure out the garlic powder, cumin, dried parsley, and za'atar seasoning onto a plate. Sprinkle these into the pan, stir, and cook for 2 to 3 minutes.

Finely chop the fresh parsley, and add the parsley and baby spinach to the pan. Gently stir the mixture for 1 minute, allowing the spinach to wilt. Squeeze in the lemon juice, if using. Serve the sausages and bell peppers with the pearl couscous.

Note: Toasting the pearl couscous adds great flavor to the dish, but it is optional. If you choose to toast the couscous, you can start to slice your bell pepper while waiting for the pan with the couscous to heat up.

Spiced Chickpeas & Zucchini with Herb Lentils

A hearty and nutritious meal like this is always welcome, and it is super flavorful as well—making it a great meal when you want something fast yet satiating. With deep flavors from cumin, paprika, and za'atar, and topped with savory yogurt sauce, it feels indulgent, too! This dish also makes an awesome meal prep; just store the yogurt sauce separately. You may want to double the yogurt recipe, as it's so scrumptious for this dish. We use sprouted lentils here, which allows for the total 15-minute cook time to work well, as the sprouted lentils cook faster than most lentils (see Note).

Servings: 3 to 4

1 cup (192 g) dried sprouted lentils (see Note)

2¼ tsp (12 g) kosher salt, divided

¼ medium red onion

3 tbsp (45 ml) olive oil

1½ medium zucchinis

3 tbsp (11 g) fresh parsley (optional)

6 tbsp (90 ml) plain, unsweetened almond-based yogurt

Juice of 1 lemon, divided

Pinch of cayenne pepper

1¼ tsp (4 g) garlic powder, divided

¾ tsp black pepper, divided

1 (15-oz [425-g]) can chickpeas, drained and rinsed

½ tsp ground cumin

1 tsp paprika, divided

2 tsp (6 g) za'atar seasoning

To make the lentils, add the lentils, 1 teaspoon of salt, and 3 cups (720 ml) of water to a medium-sized saucepan, cover, and bring it to a boil. Reduce the heat to a gentle simmer and cook the lentils, according to the package directions, until al dente. Drain away any remaining liquid.

While the lentils cook, preheat a large pan over medium heat. Thinly slice the red onion. Add it to the pan with the olive oil and 1 teaspoon of salt. Stir and cook it for 1 to 2 minutes while preparing the zucchinis. Trim the ends off the zucchinis, slice them lengthwise, then make crosswise slices ½ inch (1.3 cm) thick. Add the zucchinis to the pan, stir, and cook them for 4 to 6 minutes, stirring halfway.

Meanwhile, finely chop the fresh parsley, if using.

For the yogurt sauce, to a small bowl, add the yogurt, juice of ¼ of the lemon, cayenne, remaining ¼ teaspoon of salt, ¼ teaspoon of garlic powder, and ¼ teaspoon of black pepper to a bowl, then stir them together.

To the pan with the veggies, add the fresh parsley, chickpeas, cumin, paprika, za'atar seasoning, remaining 1 teaspoon of garlic powder, remaining ½ teaspoon of black pepper, remaining lemon juice, and the cooked lentils, and stir everything together. Serve it topped with the yogurt sauce.

Note: If you can't find sprouted lentils, canned lentils can be used. Alternatively, you can cook regular dried lentil varieties like green or black lentils, cooked to al dente, but it will extend the cooking time past 15 minutes. For the recipe, you're looking for 2⅓ cups (462 g) of cooked lentils.

Udon Noodles with Mushrooms, Tofu, & Green Beans

There's something that is just so satisfying about a plate of savory, chewy udon noodles. They take on the flavors of sauce like a dream and have that scrumptious wow factor that gets me every time. Noodles are a family favorite in our house, and my kids will often ask if I'm making them as soon as they see me starting to cook in the kitchen. Ah, if only we could eat noodles all day, every day! To save time, use thick precooked udon noodles that typically need just a couple minutes in boiled hot water, or choose dry pure soba (I say "pure" because they have more flavor than the ones that are not pure buckwheat) or rice noodles that cook in around 4 minutes.

Servings: 2 to 3

Noodles and Green Beans

2 (7-oz [198-g]) packages udon noodles (precooked, thick variety)

1½ cups (165 g) green beans, cut into thirds or fourths

7 oz (198 g) extra-firm or firm tofu

6 oz (170 g) mushrooms

2 tsp (10 ml) toasted sesame oil

½ tsp black pepper

¼ tsp garlic powder

¼ cup (12 g) chopped fresh chives

1–2 tsp (3–6 g) sesame seeds, for serving

Chili garlic sauce, for serving

Sauce

2 tsp (5 g) cornstarch

1 cup (240 ml) vegetable broth

1 tsp toasted sesame oil

1 tbsp (15 ml) hoisin sauce

1½ tbsp (23 ml) agave nectar

2½ tbsp (38 ml) soy sauce or tamari

2 tsp (10 g) ginger paste

¼ tsp garlic powder

2 tsp (10 ml) chili garlic sauce, or to taste, for spicy heat

To make the noodles, fill a large pot with 2 inches (5 cm) of water, enough to fully submerge the noodles, cover, and bring to a boil. Once boiling, add the noodles, stir, and cover again to bring to a boil. Uncover and continue to boil the noodles according to the package directions, then drain and rinse them.

Meanwhile, fill a medium saucepan with around 2 inches (5 cm) of water, cover, and bring it to a boil. Once boiling, blanch the green beans for 4 to 5 minutes until they are tender. Then drain the green beans and set them aside.

Place a large skillet over medium-high heat. Drain and gently squeeze the tofu to remove some of the water. Crumble it into the pan with your hands. Let the tofu cook while preparing the mushrooms. Finely chop the mushrooms and add them to the pan, along with the oil, pepper, and garlic powder. Cook for 6 to 8 minutes, stirring periodically.

For the sauce, to a medium bowl, add the cornstarch, broth, sesame oil, hoisin sauce, agave nectar, soy sauce, ginger paste, garlic powder, and chili garlic sauce, and whisk thoroughly to combine them.

When the mushrooms and tofu are browned, carefully pour in the sauce and let it gently bubble to thicken for 30 to 60 seconds. Add the cooked green beans, cooked noodles, and chopped chives to the pan, and stir. Serve it topped with the sesame seeds and extra chili garlic sauce, if you like it spicy!

Spicy Gochujang Tofu & Asparagus Stir-Fry

It doesn't get much simpler or more delicious than this Spicy Gochujang Tofu & Asparagus Stir-Fry! We love this spicy and savory sauce for stir-fries, as it's so simple to make while packing a big flavor punch. Gochujang makes a great pantry staple to have on hand for yummy dinners in a flash, which is perfect for what we're looking for here! You can always switch up the asparagus for a different vegetable that you may have in the fridge, making this a wonderful base recipe to use as you get creative with the ingredients! Just be sure to cut the vegetables in a manner that will ensure a quick cook.

Servings: 3 to 4

Stir-Fry
1 cup (200 g) jasmine rice
16 oz (454 g) super-firm tofu
4 tsp (20 ml) toasted sesame oil, divided
1 medium bundle asparagus
Sesame seeds, for serving
1 packed tbsp (1 g) finely chopped fresh cilantro, for serving

Sauce
3 tbsp (45 ml) gochujang
2½ tsp (25 ml) rice vinegar
3 tbsp (45 ml) water
3 tbsp (45 ml) agave nectar
¾ tsp garlic powder
¼ tsp ground ginger
1 tbsp (15 ml) soy sauce
1½ tsp (4 g) cornstarch

In a medium saucepan, add the jasmine rice plus 2 cups (480 ml) of water. Bring it to a boil, covered, then immediately reduce the heat to low and cook it until the rice is tender and the water has been absorbed, around 12 minutes.

Meanwhile, preheat a large skillet over medium-high heat. Drain the tofu and make thin slices by cutting the tofu across its depth to create four thin slabs. Make a crosswise cut across the slabs, then cut those diagonally to create triangles. Add 3 teaspoons (15 ml) of the toasted sesame oil to the pan, then place the tofu into the pan. Cook the tofu for 8 to 10 minutes, flipping it halfway. You want some browning on the tofu.

While the tofu is cooking, trim the tough bottom ends from the asparagus. Then cut them into thirds or fourths and add them to a second skillet, over medium heat, with the remaining 1 teaspoon of toasted sesame oil. Cook for 4 to 5 minutes, until they're crisp-tender, stirring periodically.

For the sauce, to a small bowl, add the gochujang, rice vinegar, water, agave nectar, garlic powder, ground ginger, soy sauce, and cornstarch, and whisk thoroughly. Then add the sauce to the tofu and cook for 1 to 2 minutes, until the sauce has thickened somewhat, gently moving the tofu pieces around slightly to let the sauce thicken and coat the pieces. Add in the asparagus, stir, then top with the sesame seeds and cilantro. Serve with the jasmine rice.

Spicy Tofu, Pepper, & Brussels Sprouts Stir-Fry

This Spicy Tofu, Pepper, & Brussels Sprouts Stir-Fry is full of spice (no surprise there!), texture, and flavor. It's also one of my favorite recipes that incorporates Brussels sprouts. They're just so delicious combined with the tofu and bell pepper in this savory, Asian-inspired sauce. The toppings also add a lot of fun to this party. We use fresh cilantro, roasted peanuts, lime, sesame seeds, and red chili flakes.

Servings: 2 to 3

Stir-Fry
16 oz (454 g) super-firm tofu

1 tbsp (15 ml) sesame oil

1 bell pepper

¼ lb (113 g) Brussels sprouts

2 packed tbsp (2 g) fresh cilantro

¼ cup (37 g) chopped roasted peanuts

¼ tsp red chili flakes

Lime wedges, for serving

2 tsp (6 g) sesame seeds, for serving (optional)

Sauce
1 tsp hoisin sauce

½ tsp garlic powder

1 tbsp (15 ml) toasted sesame oil

1 tsp cornstarch

1 tbsp (15 ml) water

1 tbsp (16 g) ginger paste

3 tbsp (45 ml) tamari

1½ tbsp (23 ml) maple syrup

1 tbsp (15 ml) lime juice (about ½ lime)

Preheat a large pan on medium-high heat. Drain the tofu, and cut it into ½-inch (1.3-cm) cubes. Add the tofu and oil to the pan. Stir and let the tofu cook while preparing the vegetables.

Thinly slice the bell pepper, then add the slices to the pan with the tofu. Stir and continue to cook the tofu and bell pepper for 5 minutes. While the tofu and bell pepper are cooking, prepare the Brussels sprouts. Cut off any rough ends, then cut them in half through the stem. Thinly slice the halved pieces, crosswise, to make "shreds." Add these to the pan, stir, and let them cook on medium heat for 1 minute.

For the sauce, to a small bowl, add the hoisin sauce, garlic powder, sesame oil, cornstarch, water, ginger paste, tamari, maple syrup, and lime juice, and whisk them together. Add the sauce to the pan, and cook it together for 1 minute. Finely chop the fresh cilantro. Serve the tofu and vegetables topped with the fresh cilantro, peanuts, red chili flakes, lime wedges, and sesame seeds if desired.

Lemon & Garlic Mixed Mushroom Stir-Fry

So many veggies, in so little time! Sorry for the bad joke, but this dish packs in a lot of veggies for a super-fast meal. The shiitake mushrooms and baby portobello mushrooms make a great pair with different bites to them, along with bell pepper and snow peas. There are chickpeas as well, for an extra fiber-filled component. Feel free to include other types of mushrooms as well, such as oyster mushrooms. This recipe uses jasmine rice to accompany the stir-fry, but a great alternative would be rice noodles or ramen noodles tossed in a touch of sesame oil.

Servings: 3 to 4

1 cup (200 g) jasmine rice

6 oz (170 g) baby portobello or cremini mushrooms

1 tbsp (15 ml) avocado oil

3.5 oz (99 g) shiitake mushrooms

½ bell pepper (see Note)

¼ lb (113 g) snow peas

3 large cloves garlic

2 tsp (5 g) cornstarch

¼ cup (60 ml) reduced-sodium soy sauce

¼ cup (60 ml) water

2 tbsp (30 ml) agave nectar

1 tbsp (15 ml) toasted sesame oil

2 tsp (10 ml) chili garlic sauce

2 tsp (10 g) ginger paste

Juice of ½ lemon

1 cup (164 g) canned chickpeas, drained and rinsed

2 tsp (6 g) sesame seeds

In a medium saucepan, add the jasmine rice plus 2 cups (480 ml) of water. Bring it to a boil, covered, then immediately reduce the heat to low and cook it until the rice is tender and the water has evaporated, around 12 minutes.

Meanwhile, preheat a large pan over medium-high heat. Slice the portobello and add them to the pan with the oil, stir, and let them cook for 1 to 2 minutes. Remove the shiitake mushroom stems and slice the caps. Add the shiitake mushrooms to the pan, stir, and let them cook for 1 minute. Dice the bell pepper, add it to the pan, stir, and let them cook for 2 minutes while preparing the snow peas.

Trim off the ends of the snow peas, and cut the remainder into thirds. Add them to the pan. Stir the vegetables and cook for another 5 minutes at medium heat, partially covered, stirring occasionally. While they are cooking, mince the garlic. In a small bowl, whisk together the cornstarch, soy sauce, water, agave nectar, sesame oil, chili garlic sauce, ginger paste, and lemon juice.

Add the garlic and chickpeas to the pan, stir, and cook for 1 minute. Add the sauce, stir, and cook for 1 minute as the sauce thickens. Serve with the jasmine rice, and top with the sesame seeds.

Note: If you would like to save some chopping effort and a bit of cooking time, you can substitute the fresh bell pepper with ½ cup (160 g) of chopped roasted red peppers. Just add them in at the end of cooking.

Rice Noodle Stir-Fry with Carrots & Shiitakes

This noodle dish is a satisfying, comfort food type of meal. We have noodles in a flavorful sauce, a delicious mix of carrots and shiitake mushrooms for your veggies, and soy curls that soak up the sauce to make it a hearty meal. I was first introduced to soy curls by a few foodie friends on Instagram, and if you haven't tried them, they're a bit of a game changer. You can find them online, and they come dry. Rehydrating them is simple; just add some hot water (or microwave them in water like we do here, to save time). If you don't have a microwave, you can heat them on the stove. Then squeeze out the water and stir-fry or sauté them, as you would vegan meat or veggies. They are great when they have a bit of browning on them, so you can adjust the heat accordingly during cooking.

Servings: 4

7 oz (198 g) rice noodles

1 cup (40 g) dry soy curls

2 medium carrots

2 tbsp (30 ml) sesame oil, divided

3.5 oz (99 g) shiitake mushrooms

6 tbsp (90 ml) soy sauce

⅔ cup (160 ml) vegetable broth

2 tbsp (30 ml) agave nectar

2 tbsp (30 ml) mirin

1 tbsp (16 g) ginger paste

2 tsp (10 ml) chili garlic sauce

1 tsp garlic powder

1 tsp cornstarch

1½ packed tbsp (2 g) fresh cilantro

1½ packed tbsp (5 g) thinly sliced scallions

Fill a large pot with 2 inches (5 cm) of water, enough to fully submerge the pasta, cover, and bring it to a boil. Once boiling, add the noodles, stir, cover, and bring it back to a boil. Then uncover and boil the pasta until it's al dente, according to the package directions. Drain and rinse the noodles.

Meanwhile, place the dry soy curls in a microwaveable bowl with enough filtered water to cover them, then heat in microwave for 2 minutes to rehydrate them. Drain and rinse them in cold water to cool down quickly, then squeeze out the excess water.

While the soy curls are rehydrating, preheat a large pan on medium heat. Thinly slice the carrots, making 1 to 2 lengthwise cuts first, depending on thickness. Add the carrots and 1 tablespoon (15 ml) of the sesame oil to the pan, along with the soy curls, and let them cook while preparing the mushrooms.

Cut the stems off the shiitake mushrooms, then slice the caps. Add these to the pan, stir, and cook for 3 to 5 minutes, until the soy curls are starting to brown, stirring periodically.

To a medium bowl, add the remaining 1 tablespoon (15 ml) of sesame oil, soy sauce, vegetable broth, agave nectar, mirin, ginger paste, chili garlic sauce, garlic powder, and cornstarch. Whisk them together, then add the sauce to the pan. Stir everything together, allowing the sauce to thicken for 30 seconds. Finely chop the cilantro, and add the cooked noodles and cilantro to the pan, and stir. Serve it by topping the noodles with the scallions.

Acknowledgments

I'd like to first thank my mom and dad for their never-ending love and encouragement, and for supporting my obsession with cooking and cooking shows throughout my childhood. They are the kindest and most enthusiastic taste testers, not to mention the best parents I could have asked for as a young cook and beyond.

Thanks to my incredible husband, Dan. You have never ceased to amaze me with your encouragement and love over all these years, and you have convinced me that so many things are indeed possible. You, Julia, and Tommy have been the best and cutest taste testers.

I'd also like to thank my amazing family and friends, including my incredible sisters, nieces, nephews, cousins, and fam across the pond. You all inspire me in different ways. To the Gibbons Girls and my NYU girls, I will forever be ecstatic that our paths crossed. To my Instagram fellow foodies, your comradery makes this journey even better.

Special thanks go to my nephew, Danny, and to Nancy R., Linda, Isabela, Cara, Kara, Nancy C., Miriam, Lindsay, Kristen, Takeenya, Krystal, Ariana, and Toni for their detailed feedback during this process.

To Sarah Monroe and the Page Street Publishing team, I can't thank you enough for believing in me and giving me this incredible opportunity and ability to bring a lifelong dream to fruition, and to share my recipes and love of plant-based food with the world and the Janet's Munch Meals online community. Your time and effort, encouragement, and guidance through this process will always be so appreciated.

I'd like to give a huge thank-you to all who have supported my recipe blog and social media, and to you, the readers of this cookbook. It makes my heart incredibly happy to know that my recipes have reached you and are part of your lives. When I see you create a recipe that I inspired, it makes my day, each and every time.

And last but certainly not least, I'd like to thank Vegan Bowls, Good Old Vegan, *Thrive Magazine*, and the *feedfeed* for their support. Without your generous sharing of my recipes along the way, I wouldn't have been able to reach the thousands of amazing followers around the world who have joined the Janet's Munch Meals Instagram and Munch Meals by Janet blog family.

About the Author

Janet Gronnow is the recipe creator and food photographer behind the popular blog Munch Meals by Janet and the @janetsmunchmeals Instagram account. Janet shares approachable, delicious meals for foodies and families, focusing on simple ingredients and preparations that pack big flavor. Her work has been featured in publications such as *Thrive Magazine* and the *feedfeed* and on the websites of Vegan Bowls and Good Old Vegan. Janet has worked with brands such as Sprouts Farmers Market, Kikkoman, Bertolli, and Treeline Cheese. When she is not creating in the kitchen, you can find Janet spending time with her beloved family, enjoying the outdoors and some good music.

Index